EARLY FOCUS

Working with Young Blind and Visually Impaired Children and Their Families

Rona L. Pogrund, Diane L. Fazzi, and Jessica S. Lampert, editors

American
Foundation
for the Blind
New York

Second printing, 1994

Printed in the United States of America

Library of Congress Cataloging-in-Publication Data

Early focus : working with young blind and visually impaired children
    and their families / edited by Rona L. Pogrund, Diane L. Fazzi, and
    Jessica S. Lampert.
        p.   cm.
    Includes bibliographical references.
    ISBN 0-89128-215-7 (alk. paper)
    1. Children, Blind--Rehabilitation. 2. Visually handicapped
children--Rehabilitation. 3. Children, Blind--Services for--United
States. 4. Visually handicapped children--Services for--United
States.   I. Pogrund, Rona L.   II. Fazzi, Diane L.   III. Lampert,
Jessica S.   IV. American Foundation for the Blind.
HV1596.5.E27   1992   92-17874
362.4'1'083--dc20   CIP

Photo credits: Blind Childrens Center, cover and pages 5, 31, 59; Diane L. Fazzi, cover and pages 95, 104; Vincent G. Fazzi, cover and pages 24, 26, 29, 41, 55, 77, 78, 83, 101, 103, 109, 110, 115, 125.

This publication is based on a joint project of California State University, Los Angeles, and the Foundation for the Junior Blind, Los Angeles, California, funded by personnel preparation grant #G008630011-88 from the Office of Special Education Programs, U.S. Department of Education, March 1, 1986-February 28, 1989.

To our families and all families
who provide love, guidance, support,
and life focus . . .
and to those special people
who helped us
through this project
with their enduring patience.

CONTENTS

FOREWORD

Providing very young visually impaired children with programs of stimulation and support takes substantial specialized skill, especially when those children have more than one disability. The expertise needed to meet unique needs comes from many disciplines brought together in a transdisciplinary fashion. Because of this, *Early Focus: Working with Young Blind and Visually Impaired Children and Their Families* is an important resource for professionals and parents alike. Based on training institutes co-sponsored by the Foundation for the Junior Blind in Los Angeles and California State University, Los Angeles, the book synthesizes and makes understandable the experience and knowledge of professionals from fields as diverse as education, orientation and mobility, pediatrics, ophthalmology and optometry, psychology, occupational therapy, and social work. Anyone concerned with children who are blind or visually impaired will find valuable information here.

In addition to crossing the boundaries of many disciplines, *Early Focus* crosses the boundaries of culture and ethnic identity. In line with our mission at the American Foundation for the Blind to promote independence and services for all visually impaired people, the book includes material specifically addressing issues related to cultural sensitivity and to work with families from various minority groups.

Early Focus is a pioneering effort in spotlighting the issues facing people who work with visually impaired children in their extremely formative years. We hope that this collection of expert perspectives helps lay the groundwork for continued efforts.

Carl R. Augusto
President and Executive Director
American Foundation for the Blind

PREFACE

Because of the increased incidence of visual impairments among infants, toddlers, and preschoolers, the demand for both public and private agencies to serve young visually impaired children is increasing significantly as well. Currently, many orientation and mobility specialists and teachers of children with visual impairments do not feel qualified to meet the needs of this special population and their families adequately. With the 1986 passage of P.L. 99-457, the amendments to the Education for All Handicapped Children Act (now called the Individuals with Disabilities Education Act), special education services have been expanded to children of preschool age with disabilities, with greater incentives offered for serving the 0–3-year-old population.

Concern about the growing prevalence of young visually impaired children has mounted since the 1980s. According to a statistical analysis conducted by the American Foundation for the Blind (Uslan, 1983), the number of legally blind children from birth to age 5 was predicted to increase by 19 percent from 1980 to 1990, to a projected total of 8,200 legally blind children. These statistics do not even include the many children with low vision who do not qualify for definition as legally blind or those with multiple disabilities not identified due to the unduplicated child counts in which visually impaired children with other disabilities are included only under a disability category other than visual impairment. The 1990 American Printing House for the Blind pupil count showed a 94.13 percent increase in the visually impaired infant population and a 79.35 percent increase in the preschool-age population from 1984 to 1990. As of this writing, no later statistics are available, but the numbers are expected to continue rising into the 1990s. Uslan (1983) also indicated that the future training needs of specialists in the visual impairment field should include an emphasis on work with this very young population.

A primary factor accounting for the increase in visually impaired infants is the increased survival rate among premature infants. More low-birthweight infants (approximately 1–3 pounds [500-1,500 grams]) have been surviving because of technological advances in neonatal care. These infants, however, often have a variety of disabling conditions, and there is currently a resurgence of retinopathy of prematurity (ROP), formerly known as retrolental fibroplasia (RLF), among these surviving infants (Morse & Trief, 1985). Professionals estimate that more than 2,000 newborn infants annually will develop some degree of ROP, 23 percent of them severely visually impaired or totally blind. The incidence of ROP increases as birthweight decreases (Trief, Duckman, Morse, & Silberman, 1989). Keith and Kitchens (1983) found a 33 percent incidence of ocular defects in babies with very low birthweights. Four possible factors placing a child at risk of developing a visual impairment are prematurity, a family history of a visual defect, infection during pregnancy, and difficult or assisted labor.

Many other visual impairments also affect newborn infants. These may include congenital cataracts, glaucoma, retinoblastoma, retinitis pigmentosa, and optic-nerve hypoplasia. The increase in teenage pregnancy has also increased the incidence of premature births, lower birthweights, and such congenital neurological impairments as deafness and blindness (Schinke, Gilchrist, & Small, 1979). Later maternal age increases complications in labor, toxemia, and the occurrence of Down's syndrome—all of which increase the chance of visual impairment in the newborn.

The number of infants born with multiple disabilities is on the rise as well. Twenty-five percent of the deaf population have a visual impairment, and 50 percent of individuals with cerebral palsy have some kind of visual deficiency (Cross, 1981). In addition, the increase in the use by pregnant women of a variety of drugs has further affected the number of infants being born with visual and other impairments. Meeting the needs of drug-exposed infants may be one of the greatest challenges facing the field of special education over the next decade.

Traditionally, personnel preparation programs have not addressed the unique programmatic aspects of serving visually impaired infants in the depth and manner that are now required. Thus many visually impaired newborns and infants went unserved or were served in generic special education programs without personnel trained in meeting their specialized needs. Recently, however, several degree programs in the education of blind and visually impaired infants, toddlers, and preschoolers have been developed to provide such in-depth training. Previously, the personnel preparation programs for orientation and mobility specialists and for teachers of visually impaired children addressed the infant and preschool population only minimally within the required coursework; time limitations did not allow for in-depth study of, and practicum experiences with, members of this young population and their families. To address the need for intensified training in this area, a model was developed for a federal grant project, funded by a personnel preparation grant from the Office of Special Education Programs, Office of Special Education and Rehabilitation Services, U.S. Department of Education, in the form of three-week intensive summer training institutes held during the summers of 1986, 1987, and 1988. The project, entitled "Training Personnel to Serve Visually Impaired and Multihandicapped Infants and Their Families," was co-sponsored by California State University, Los Angeles, and the Foundation for the Junior Blind, Los Angeles.

Sixty-two trainees (20 or 21 per year) participated on a full-time basis during the three-week summer institutes over the three-year period. Most of the trainees were preservice orientation and mobility specialists, teachers of children with visual impairments, or early childhood specialists interested in working with young visually impaired children. The participants met from 9:00 A.M. to 4:00 P.M., Monday through Friday, for three weeks and received intensive training in how to work with this population of young children with visual impairments. They heard many expert speakers, made observation visits to a variety of programs for young visually impaired children, had hands-on practicum experiences with infants and preschoolers and their parents, and participated in many activities. There was a strong emphasis on family involvement and on work in a transdisciplinary team to meet the needs of these children more effectively. In addition to the full participants each year, more than 200 other professionals, parents, and other interested persons attended some or all of the speakers' presentations.

The high caliber of the presentations made by the speakers at the institutes and the outstanding synthesis offered of current theory and research, best practices, and relevant information inspired the development of this publication. Each presentation was videotaped; then selected presentations that were thought to be of national interest were summarized so that relevant content could be presented in written format for publication as proceedings from the institutes. It was felt that the content of the presentations would be valuable to preservice teachers, professionals in the field, parents, and other interested individuals. These summaries have been compiled, merged, supplemented, and edited in an effort to share the outstanding expertise of the speakers who participated in the project. In addition, the editors authored material on some of the topics in the book not covered by them in the institutes in an effort to provide a comprehensive publication on early childhood visual impairment.

As coordinator of the project, I could not have carried out the summer institutes without the tremendous help of many other people. A very special thank-you goes to my three project co-directors from the Foundation for the Junior Blind—Jenny Boyd, Jessica Lampert, and Sheila Wolfe—each of whom contributed significantly to the success of the project. Thanks are also due Kay Clarke, who helped create the concept of the institutes and assisted in the development of the original grant proposal. Special acknowledgment and gratitude go to Diane Fazzi and Jessica Lampert, my co-editors, for the many hours of work they put into this publication. Jessica Lampert initially summarized the speakers' videotapes, and Diane Fazzi worked with me diligently in the editing, writing, and rewriting. Special thanks are extended to Margie Moennich and Maria Gutierrez for their many hours of clerical assistance in the preparation of this book. I would also like to express my gratitude to Bob Ralls and the staff at the Foundation for the Junior Blind who gave the project their ongoing support. I am grateful to Vince Fazzi for his time and effort in photographing pictures for this book and to the Blind Childrens Center and the Azusa Unified School District for their cooperation and assistance regarding the taking of pictures. Appreciation goes to all the many agencies, parents, and professionals who contributed to the summer institutes over the three years through such efforts as allowing observations and helping with hands-on experiences. The project truly stands as a model of collaboration between higher education and community agencies. A final note of thanks is expressed to each of the consultants on the project who served as a presenter.

At this point, a comment about appropriate settings for blind and visually impaired children is in order. The editors of this volume do not advocate any one kind of placement—disability-specific classes, integrated classrooms, or segregated programs—as appropriate for all children. However, we do philosophically believe that a disability-specific program in the early years is the best placement for many young visually impaired children if they are to succeed in more integrated settings later. This philosophy does not preclude integration with sighted children nor exclude any program option as inappropriate. The individual needs of the child are the determining factor in regard to appropriateness of placement.

The original purpose of the summer training institutes was to improve the preparation of personnel for work with visually impaired and multiply impaired infants and preschoolers and their families. There are now many more teachers who will be more knowledgeable about meeting the needs of this growing population. It is hoped that by disseminating the information derived from the institutes further through this publication, an even greater number of professionals and parents will be able to meet the unique needs of this group of young visually impaired children more effectively.

Rona L. Pogrund

Chapter 1

FAMILY FOCUS: WORKING WITH FAMILIES OF YOUNG BLIND AND VISUALLY IMPAIRED CHILDREN

CONTRIBUTORS

Renee A. Cohen
Family Issues—Professional Viewpoint

Lois Harrell
Hospitalization Issues

Cheryl I. Macon
Cultural Issues
Working with Black Families

Sri J. Moedjono
Cultural Issues
Working with Asian Families

Linda S. Orrante
Cultural Issues
Working with Hispanic Families

Rona L. Pogrund
Communication Strategies

Patricia Sacks Salcedo
Family Issues—Parental Viewpoint
Transition Issues

In the belief that the family is the most significant influence in the life of a visually impaired child, this book starts with a focus on the family. The young visually impaired child cannot be viewed as an entity unto him- or herself but must be seen as part of an interactive family system. The professional's effectiveness in working with young visually impaired children is increased by a family-centered philosophy. Professionals working with visually impaired children will have a greater impact if they have an understanding of, sensitivity toward, and respect for the family.

The image of the two-parent family with the father as "breadwinner" and the mother who stays at home to care for the children and the house is no longer a true representation of American society (Thorp & Brown, 1987). The American family portrait must be expanded to include working mothers, families separated by divorce, "blended" families or stepfamilies, homosexual partners, single parents, grandparents as primary caregivers, unwed teenage mothers, and adoptive and foster families.

Early childhood specialists need to be increasingly sensitive to these current family structures when collaborating in the design and implementation of early intervention programs. All such strategies should reflect the individual family's values, concerns, priorities, and cultural background. Integrating an understanding of unique family structures and other family characteristics into the intervention process will in all likelihood result in a greater impact on the child's overall development.

This chapter outlines grief and coping cycles and individual reactions associated with the birth of a visually impaired child. It discusses professional responses, including supportive communication, active listening, and information sharing. Families of visually impaired infants go through many transitions, including the hospital experience, the hospital-to-home transition, the home-to-school transition, and the school-to-school transition. Suggestions are made to assist professionals in supporting families through these transitions. Cultural considerations are presented to help professionals become more sensitive when working with families.

EMOTIONAL REACTIONS OF FAMILIES

The birth of a visually impaired child upsets the equilibrium of the family, bringing forth a multitude of emotions. Such a birth symbolizes the loss of the perfect child and of the parents' self-esteem. It has been suggested that families go through a specific sequence of feelings very similar to the grief cycle—typically including the stages of shock, denial, guilt, anger, depression, objectivity, and resolution—felt by people experiencing a major loss, as illustrated by the traditional model in Figure 1. Others suggest that individual family members do not adhere to orderly, sequential, predictable reactions. Individuals may go through the stages of reactions countless times in varying orders, expending different amounts of time and energy at each stage, and they may skip some stages altogether. Indeed, many parents comment that specific events trigger all or parts of the cycle. The emotional responses of families are too complex to classify into absolute, rigid stages, as suggested by the revised and individualized models in Figure 1. Human behavior does not always follow a clinical model.

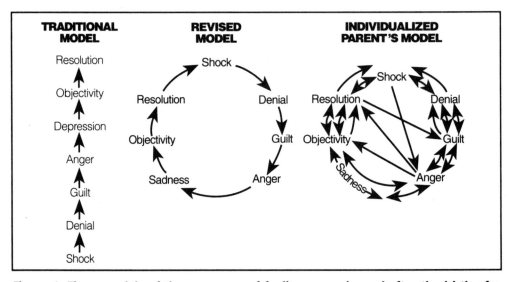

Figure 1. Three models of the sequence of feelings experienced after the birth of a visually impaired child.

It is important to be sensitive to a family's current emotional state and equally important to avoid categorizing family members according to predetermined expectations that accompany more traditional models. At any given point, families need opportunities to express themselves, and they need acknowledgment of their feelings by others. They also need specific, relevant information regarding their child, presented in an honest, empathic manner.

The individuality of the emotional reactions of families is highlighted by Patricia Salcedo (1986) in her following comments on her feelings as a parent of a visually impaired child when the child was three years old:

> *Shock* came first in my particular experience. I felt as if I were outside the window looking in. Surely this prevented my jumping through the window.
>
> I decided to skip *Denial* as previously arranged. This resulted in "over-handicapping" my child. I could not see her strengths because I was overwhelmed with her weaknesses. However, in dealing with those weaknesses, I set up a very comprehensive intervention program. The benefits of this program have been worth the emotional cost to me.
>
> "Let's skip *Guilt*, too," I thought. This has been a well-orchestrated pregnancy. Daily quarts of milk began two months before conception. We didn't even sit in the smoking section of restaurants. I know that I could not have prevented my child's birth defects. I also felt no guilt in choosing to bring her home from the hospital and raise her.
>
> *Anger*, however, consumed me. Anger against people in the supermarket. Anger against insensitive doctors. Anger against my elder daughter when she spilled milk. Anger against the neighbors with normal children. Anger against the President of the United States. It knew no bounds. Some anger lay outside of the coping process. (Some professionals blame all anger on the coping process, as if it were illegitimate or an alien feeling.) Slowly, it weakened. Occasionally, it stirs deep inside.
>
> *Sadness* follows, theoretically. Sadness deserves its own circle in the coping diagram. It accompanies all the other stages. Sadness surfaces when we fail to reach developmental milestones. It surfaces when we do reach them, often because of the pain and extended effort our kids spent achieving them. It occurs on birthdays, at surgeries, with rude remarks, and with developmental testing. I feel pain when I realize my child will always be different in a world unaccepting of difference.
>
> Pushing sadness away requires continual effort. One positive outcome— bonding easily with other parents of impaired children. We understand each other's pain. *This* is coping.
>
> *Objectivity* should follow. We parents must be objective. We are the responsible party. Objectivity can be hard to define. Professionals and parents may disagree while both claiming to be "objective." In the coping process, however, such a stage is vital. After the tears, we need to assess what we must do: which services are necessary, what medical advice is valid.
>
> *Resolution*. We felt it Day One: love, responsibility, acceptance. We had nowhere to go but up. Our family bonded tightly. Trauma came with other people's lack of "Resolution." On good days, I feel as I did at my child's birth. It's a "high" that is difficult to maintain. We walk a fine line—accepting our children's limitations yet pushing them toward an unknown potential.
>
> *Guilt* caught up with me. When my child was two years old, she required emergency surgery. Why had I missed the symptoms (why had the doctors missed the symptoms)? The signs were unobservable, yet I punished myself for not finding them.
>
> *Denial*, too, sneaks in. As my child grows, the finality of her limitations looms. I fight this. A little can't hurt—it allows me to try one more time.

RESPONSES OUTSIDE THE IMMEDIATE FAMILY

Although the emotions of the family at the birth of a visually impaired child may be tumultuous, it is not uncommon for friends, members of the extended family, and medical and other professional personnel to respond to families by denying their feelings in a variety of ways. Denial of their feelings can exacerbate parents' confusion and pain during the diagnosis period. Statements such as, "You're never given more than you can handle," "I'm sure there's a specialist somewhere who can give you a second opinion," "You're just saying that because you're stressed," or "What are you going to do now?" are all roadblocks to communication that make a person in pain feel unheard and uncared for.

When relatives, friends, and professionals can acknowledge the family's feelings, they can be more supportive by responding with statements such as, "It sounds like you're feeling a great deal of pain," "You must be feeling confused and overwhelmed now," or "You may be feeling scared because you don't know what to expect." These types of validating statements should be accompanied by sensitive listening and emotional support when the family wants it.

Professionals should always listen empathically first and then provide information when they know what is needed and relevant to a particular family at a particular time. By listening actively in an attempt to understand family concerns, professionals allow families to utilize their own strengths to solve problems that are a priority for them. Active listening involves reflecting back or paraphrasing what a person says or what you think he or she feels to verify understanding. This communication skill demonstrates empathy. If unsolicited by the family, even well-intentioned professional advice may not lead to a resolution of a difficulty. Advice giving may communicate a lack of trust in the other person's capabilities. Families are most likely to implement actions they have personally determined to be important.

SUPPORTIVE COMMUNICATION

Professionals who work with families of visually impaired infants can learn more positive communication strategies. Establishing a climate in which supportive communication can take place provides the foundation for improved understanding and increased problem solving.

According to Combs (1980), the elements of a supportive climate include the following: (1) empathy, which conveys respect for others' thoughts and feelings, (2) spontaneity, which facilitates the open expression of thoughts and feelings, (3) problem solving, which reflects openness to a collaborative resolution, and (4) synergy, which results in a mutually satisfying solution. To facilitate a supportive environment, other factors should also be present: (1) genuine desire to communicate with others; if the desire is not genuine, others can tell and will not feel free to communicate, (2) careful and attentive listening, and (3) a sharing of one's own perspective with others, with a shift of thinking at times.

Supportive communication means moving from thinking in terms of preconceived answers to thinking in terms of the desired end results and seeking solutions to meet those ends. To establish supportive communication, professionals can use the following tips on sharing information:

Supportive communication between families and professionals can help lead to positive interactions between parent and child.

- Relevant information, not advice, should be provided.
- Individuals should be in the company of a trusted relative or friend when given a medical or developmental diagnosis.
- More than one opportunity for sharing information and asking questions should be provided to families under stress.
- To increase understanding, information should be presented in a variety of ways.
- Information should be shared in a sensitive manner.
- Information should be provided from a culturally relevant perspective and in language understandable by the family.
- In information sharing, parents should be encouraged to use direct communication in expressing their concerns and priorities.
- Families should be assisted in preparing questions and observational information to present to medical personnel.
- Note taking or tape recording can help some families process technical or complicated information or can be used to share information with family members who are not present.
- Professionals should treat family members as individuals.
- Brothers and sisters of visually impaired children should be given accurate information and should be encouraged to talk openly about their feelings.

SUPPORTING FAMILIES THROUGH TRANSITIONS

Certain times in a child's life represent changes for the entire family. These transitions may be stressful for all families and may present additional challenges for the families of visually impaired children.

The Hospital Experience

Hospitalization can have a negative impact on anyone, but the often-lengthy stays involving complicated medical procedures that are not uncommon following the birth of a visually impaired child can exhaust parents and disrupt family life. For the premature infant with retinopathy of prematurity, the hospital experience can be prolonged for months due to associated neonatal care. Children with congenital cataracts and glaucoma may experience multiple corrective surgeries very early in life.

Families of visually impaired infants will often have to interact with large numbers of medical personnel, whose involvement with them often changes on an hourly or daily basis. These individuals may have different perspectives and may vary greatly in interpersonal skills. During this time, families may try to juggle their daily routines while spending long hours at the hospital. All these factors may contribute to increased emotional—and financial—strain on the family.

Hospital-to-Home Transition

Issues associated with the hospital-to-home transition for the family of a visually impaired infant may include:

- Ongoing caretaking responsibility becomes the central family focus in the case of fragile infants with extensive medical needs.
- Social contacts and activities are often reduced due to the discomfort—based on stereotypes about blindness—of friends and relatives.
- Increased isolation results in reduced social supports for the family.
- Medical procedures (such as putting eyedrops in the infant's eyes, inserting contact lenses, patching, and suctioning) may be difficult to implement at home.
- When procedures are not followed precisely, sometimes in response to the child's discomfort or protest, parents may feel guilty.
- The family must adjust to caring for the baby's medical needs without the immediate support of the child's doctors and nurses.
- The family may have concerns regarding the balance between employment and child care. These can be complicated when considering the needs of a visually impaired infant.
- The family will need to learn a whole new vocabulary of medical and educational jargon in order to communicate effectively with professionals.
- The family will need to familiarize themselves with available community resources and will need to schedule additional medical and professional services within the family routine from such practitioners as ophthalmologists, physical therapists, infant-vision specialists, and orientation and mobility specialists.
- The family may need to develop advocacy strategies to ensure community services are provided for their child.

Home-to-School Transition

When the visually impaired child reaches preschool age, many new issues may become important:

- If the child has been served by a home-based program, the family may face losing contact with a teacher whom they know and trust and with whom they feel comfortable.

- If the child is to begin a school-based program, the family will have to deal with teachers and routines they do not know and possibly with teachers who are unfamiliar with their child's disability; they may find themselves "settling" for certain conditions, acknowledging that no one can care for their child as much or as well as they do.

- With the start of a school program, parents may lose control over many aspects of the child's life that were central to the home routine; if the child is nonverbal, parents may lose contact with portions of the child's activities during the day.

- The family may also be forced to deal with the bureaucracy of the school system in general and the special education system specifically. Parents must become familiar with the policies, procedures, and options available to them.

- Transportation to and from school must be addressed. The family may be concerned about the child's riding a bus, the length of the ride, or the child's safe arrival at school or at home.

School-to-School Transition

As the visually impaired child changes schools and moves from one classroom to another, many of the issues involved in the home-to-school transition remain relevant. In addition, parents must deal with new situations:

- If the visually impaired child is placed on an integrated campus, the child and family must deal with the curiosity of other children and adults.

- The family may find themselves expending a great deal of energy in educating the new teachers about their visually impaired child, in securing necessary services for their child, and in ensuring continuity of services from one setting to another.

Helping Strategies

Professionals working with families in transition can help in a variety of ways. The following suggestions may facilitate smoother transitions:

- Encourage the family to have face-to-face meetings with the child's new teachers; the teacher and the family may feel more comfortable with each other if they meet before the first day of school.

- Provide in-service training to the school staff and information to classmates about the visually impaired child, the disability's implications, and available support and resources.

- Provide resource contacts in writing to the family as well as to the staff; the name of a contact person is often helpful.

- Apprise the family of applicable laws and of rights and services available. Although the family may not utilize all the information offered at the time, they may refer to it as needed in the future.

- Provide formal or informal advocacy training for the family, possibly role playing difficult situations and anticipating problems and responses to them.
- Encourage parent-professional collaboration. Inform families of educational and support meetings where collaboration can occur.
- If possible, provide contact with other families of visually impaired children for support purposes.

It is important to remember that it is always the family's choice to act or not to act on the information provided by the professional. Parent-professional relationships in which there exists mutual respect are the most beneficial to all parties involved.

CULTURAL CONSIDERATIONS

Awareness of and sensitivity toward the unique characteristics of a variety of cultures foster more effective work with families of a given culture. This discussion presents information about cultural considerations that are especially important when home-based services for young visually impaired children are provided; it is based primarily on the personal experiences of contributors to this chapter, who are representatives of their respective cultures.

Asian Families

Asians comprise the largest group of immigrants now in the process of coming to the United States. Approximately 30 distinct ethnic groups have immigrated to America from Asia. Within this diversity, certain commonalities seem to exist.

The family is the most important unit within the Asian culture. The individual is expected to conform to familial and societal values. Cooperation, obligation, and reciprocity are essential elements of social interaction.

The man is considered to be the head of most Asian households. Occupying the dominant position within the patriarchal family, he is the primary decision maker. Women are responsible for the family's well-being, including the teaching of moral and ethical values. They are primary caregivers for the children (Yano, 1986).

By Western standards, Asian parents tend to be very tolerant, permissive, and quick to gratify the infant's early dependency needs. Asian families do not adhere to rigid feeding and sleeping schedules for their infants and do not have early expectations for the reaching of developmental milestones such as weaning, toileting, and self-feeding. It is not uncommon for young children to sleep in the same bed as their parents. Parents view the infant as a helpless individual; they are total providers. Close contact with the infant is considered to be extremely important, and mother-infant interactions are characterized by close physical contact rather than an emphasis on vocal exchange. Early-interventionists need to be sensitive to this value when attempting to promote increased vocalizations with the visually impaired infant.

Although the Asian infant may receive immediate gratification, as the child grows older he or she is expected to assume responsibilities. By school age, there is a contrast between what appears to have been a very relaxed early childhood and the strict rearing practices of later childhood. The child is expected to acquire and assume responsibility quickly for self-help skills and preacademics.

As a general rule, during interactions with the child in the family, the parent speaks and the child listens. Often, parents expect unquestioning obedience from their children, and children are taught to refrain from expressing emotion. Everything a child does reflects on the family. This family value may be in direct conflict with many early intervention curricula, which emphasize two-way social interactions. Furthermore, when a child accomplishes something, rather than offering praise, parents may encourage him or her to accomplish more.

Frequently viewed as the consequence of some past action, a disabled child may be considered a stigma within the community. Often the feeling is that the parent has committed a sin, that something happened to the mother during pregnancy, or that the baby was "possessed" at birth. Another traditional belief attributes disabling conditions to an imbalance (excess or deficiency) in physiological functions, the principle being that health is maintained when the forces of yin and yang and the "five elements" of the body are balanced and in harmony. As such, the family may seek a cure for their child's visual impairment from a traditional healer within the community; this may delay the process of coming to acceptance and working with the child. Members of Asian cultures may have a firm belief in fate and may not experience a grief cycle similar to that discussed in the clinical models of Western culture.

Traditional Asian culture may affect group interactions in that individuals may believe that they must have harmony in their lives and that conflict is to be avoided. Many Asians do not openly disagree with an authority figure or express an opinion. They often attempt to avoid hostility of any kind.

The tradition of unquestioning confidence in authority figures may affect the family-professional relationship. Although teachers may be highly respected, their credibility may be diminished within the family if they overtly contradict traditional Asian values. Asian families may not directly express opinions or disagreement with the professional. Instead, they may simply ignore recommendations and avoid appointments and future communications. Asian families may not always seek professional assistance, but when they do, they place responsibility with the professional for whatever is within the professional's domain and therefore may feel uncomfortable participating in parent-professional conferences and the development of educational plans. In turn, the professional must recognize the family as the primary social unit within the culture and the traditional role of senior family members in collectively providing input, making decisions, and resolving problems as they relate to the individual within the family.

In general, Asian families have a sense of obligation to and reciprocity with anyone who helps their children, and the debt owed is viewed as lifelong. Their gratitude is displayed through gift giving or personalized expressions of repayment (that is, invitations to family affairs or events). Refusal to accept a family's offer of gifts, favors, or invitations may be construed as rejection and an insult to the family. Considerable tact and sensitivity are called for in such situations.

Strategies for Working with Asian Families

Observance of a few rules of social conduct may facilitate the process of getting acquainted with and accepted by the Asian family:

- Asian families as a rule do not address professionals by their first names.
- Bowing or putting hands together and bowing is a common form of greeting instead of a handshake.
- It is considered impolite to show the soles of one's shoes. It is important to be aware of the position of one's feet. Pointing with one's toe is considered disrespectful.
- "Wisdom comes with age" is given much credence. Older professionals may gain trust and respect more readily than younger professionals.
- Work with the child in the presence of the family; if there are senior family members available, ask for their participation in the child's intervention.
- In many Asian cultures it is considered to be bad luck to touch an infant on the head.
- Fleeting eye contact with strangers is more comfortable than direct eye-to-eye contact.
- Asian individuals may sometimes smile or laugh to avoid dealing with true feelings, thus avoiding conflict.

Black Families

Black Americans may come from highly diverse locations including Africa, the Caribbean, and Central and South America. As with members of any racial or ethnic population, it is essential to view each family individually because generalizations may not be accurate. Family structures vary according to the cultural background of the particular family. It is important to determine the family composition when initiating intervention.

The black family is probably the most flexible of family systems in the American culture. There is a unique kinship bond among black families, which are often multigenerational. Thus the extended family plays a significant role in connecting a number of households.

The church, which provides support and comfort, is traditionally an important part of the black family, and African traditions may be passed from generation to generation through the Gospel. It is not uncommon for the family to consult with the pastor or for the pastor to be considered a part of the family.

Single-parent families are not uncommon in black communities, and this family structure is often forced on families by stipulations relating to available public financial assistance. Many black children could not receive such assistance if an unemployed father resided within the home. This constraint does not preclude the involvement with the family of those black fathers who do not live with their children. Even if the father is not available, there is often a male authority figure in the family who may be a boyfriend, uncle, grandfather, or other relative or friend. Single-parent families place a heavy reliance on "inter-household kinship systems" for emotional and financial support (Mullings-Franco, 1987).

Child-rearing practices vary from family to family. In some families several people may take responsibility for the child, including older brothers and sisters. There may not be distinct role delineations like those that exist in other cultures. Individuality is valued highly. Black children are encouraged to be autonomous by expressing their personality and determining their environment. Regular feeding schedules are generally considered unimportant within the context of the family. Members of the extended family hold, cuddle, and talk to the infant, and there is an emphasis on human interactions as opposed to exploration of the environment. Toys are considered to be of less importance than human contact (Mullings-Franco, 1987).

For the most part, if the black family is upwardly mobile and economically well established, the fact that a child is visually impaired may be perceived as a great problem and a cause for concern, and intervention is likely to be desired. In contrast, families of a lower economic class who may be struggling for survival may not find a child's visual impairment to be a high-priority concern in relation to other family-life issues. Black families may experience varying levels of guilt concerning a child's visual impairment, possibly associating impairment with some prior wrongdoing. It would not be uncommon for visually impaired children to be protected by the extended family or by the greater community at large.

Strategies for Working with Black Families

Familiarity with the following strategies and factors may be useful when working with black families with young visually impaired children:

- Time concepts within black cultures may be different from those of the majority culture, and some families may not strictly adhere to timetables and schedules; it may be helpful to call ahead when planning a home visit.
- Some families may prefer to be identified by nationality rather than by race.
- Many families live in unsafe neighborhoods or housing projects; often, however, the service provider will become known in the community and will be protected.
- When communicating with black families, clarify any terminology of "black English" if it is unfamiliar. One should not assume that if a family does not use standard English they are uneducated.
- There is often a lack of trust of the service provider, so rapport should be established with the family before work with the child is attempted.

Hispanic Families

By the end of the 20th century, as a result of the rapid growth of their numbers, Hispanics will be the largest minority group in the United States. The birthrate for Hispanics is higher than that of the general population. Contributing additionally to the rapid growth rate is a continuous migration to the United States from Latin American countries.

Hispanic families come to the United States from Mexico, Cuba, Puerto Rico, and all Central and South American countries, bringing with them varied experiences and cultures. It is important to realize that there is a great diversity among the Hispanic population, and it is impossible to characterize accurately all Hispanics as a group. Hispanics as a group do share certain linguistic and cultural characteristics, but *Hispanic* is an umbrella term that encompasses people with very distinct political, economic, and racial differences.

The extended family is the key source of support in the Hispanic community. The family is considered more important than the individual, and the individual's needs come after the family's. The individual family member is a representative of the family, and the family is the source of individual identity.

The father is typically the head of the household and the authority figure. In most families, few decisions are made without the father's knowledge and approval. Generally, the father is not emotionally expressive and may appear somewhat aloof, reserved, and independent from other family members. He may be very close to, and affectionate with, his young children but markedly less demonstrative as they approach adulthood. The mother's role is typically to be devoted to her husband and children, to provide emotional support to her husband, and to take care of the home. Traditionally, her needs come last, and she is expected to make any sacrifice necessary for the family. The mother is the nurturer of the family, even as the children grow older. Generally, the Hispanic mother is highly respected, almost revered, for her role in the family.

These traditional roles are no longer so widely accepted by Hispanic women today. Many women are less willing to carry out these expected duties and may feel pressure from American society to incorporate more nontraditional female roles into their behavior. In addition, in many instances women may be experiencing increased opportunities for employment, while Hispanic males may often be subject to fewer job opportunities, thus creating potential conflict within the family.

Although parents may often be permissive and indulgent with their children in the early years, frivolous or disrespectful behavior is not accepted. Children are given real responsibilities within the family, including the care of younger sisters and brothers. Typically the son's role is to learn to be a good husband, and he is given a great deal of freedom within the family and encouraged to be independent. Sons are expected to look after their sisters, even if the sisters are several years older. If the father is absent, and there are no adult male relatives to take over, the oldest son assumes the father's roles and duties. The daughter is traditionally very protected within the family, and her traditional role is to learn to be a wife and mother.

Within this culture, the family assumes primary responsibility for the care of its disabled members and will do so at home if at all possible. One of the main purposes of the family is to care for its members in time of need. A family member's disability may disrupt the equilibrium of a family already barely managing to make ends meet, thus upsetting the delicate balance of everyday survival.

The visually impaired child may be indulged, spoiled, or most likely pitied. The child may be treated as special and, in some cases, may become functionally more disabled than he or she actually is as a result of not being permitted to function in appropriate family roles. The mother and other family members may experience profound guilt and feel that the child's disability is a punishment from God for some act the mother committed. Often a disabled son will be a great disappointment, especially for the father, who may withdraw from the child. The child may be treated as if he did not exist; it may be easier for the father to withdraw rather than think of the son as a poor reflection of himself. In this case the father's expectations and aspirations will reside with another child. A disabled girl, as a young child, will bear a special disadvantage, as not as much is expected from the daughter in a Hispanic household.

If they are extremely religious, Hispanic parents may not observably express all the emotions of the coping cycle. To do so would be considered inappropriate or in conflict with "God's will." Hispanic families often accept the fact that a child has a disability. Frequently, they are less interested in academic performance and independence than in social competence (Eagar, 1987). Parents may be less concerned about early intervention for the child with low vision who is functioning successfully at home within a social context, as other areas of functioning may be considered a low priority. The child's ability to behave appropriately is often a higher priority than success in other areas of development, and this and related beliefs may prompt a decreased sense of urgency in implementation of intervention strategies.

Strategies for Working with Hispanic Families

The following strategies and factors may be helpful to consider when working with Hispanic families with young visually impaired children:

- Traditional cultural mores dictate that babies should be touched by visitors, especially by unmarried women, to avoid *mal ojo* (the evil eye).
- Accept courtesies the family offers, such as food. Often the offering of these is a matter of pride to the family, and nonacceptance could be insulting.
- Be sensitive to the Hispanic perception of time. Punctuality may not be a priority and in fact is often considered rude.
- Because an older sister may be the primary caregiver for a visually impaired child, she should be involved in the intervention process (that is, by learning techniques, activities, positioning, and so on).

Cross-Cultural Strategies

Sensitivity to, and understanding of, the family's cultural values and context enhance the professional's effectiveness as a service provider. A number of cross-cultural strategies may be particularly helpful:

- It is important that service providers examine their own feelings about members of different ethnic groups. Self-awareness is the first step to effective communication.
- Determine the family's cultural assimilation by talking with family members and observing attitudes and behaviors.
- It is imperative to take time to get to know the family and their traditions and values and to defer getting into details of the workplan for the child until rapport with the family is established.

- Remember that each family is a unique and dynamic system that has to be defined in its own right.
- Take time to establish trust with the family. Talk with children present, and interact with the family in a personal yet professional manner.
- It may be helpful to identify a respected senior member of the community or family for assistance in gaining acceptance by the family.
- Remember to make positive comments about the family and child.
- If appropriate, tell the family something about yourself to make interactions more personal.
- Limit the use of educational jargon in written and oral communications when working with the family.
- Allow the family to arrange seating; it may demonstrate which family members have greatest influence or importance.
- The family may not question professionals even when there is disagreement; it is important to help members of the family raise questions.
- Consider using a bilingual service provider when working with a monolingual family. Although this is not an automatic open door, it often helps. Using children or related adults as interpreters may be limiting in that they may not interpret clearly or may add their own agenda to the communication.
- It is important to help the family build skills so they can function without the service provider.
- Offer choices to the family, expressing clearly what the available choices are. Help the family learn how to "use the system." Advocate for them in front of them, and help them find a way to deal with the system that is comfortable for them.

These suggested strategies may provide a general framework for cultural considerations. It is, however, important to determine to what extent each individual family has become assimilated into the American culture. Second- or third-generation families may be more likely to have adopted nontraditional values and life-styles. Part of being culturally sensitive is avoiding the assumption that families maintain all traditional cultural values. Approaching families with a nonjudgmental, open mind and taking time to observe and listen may be the most effective strategies of all.

Chapter 2

VISION FOCUS: UNDERSTANDING THE MEDICAL AND FUNCTIONAL IMPLICATIONS OF VISION LOSS IN YOUNG BLIND AND VISUALLY IMPAIRED CHILDREN

CONTRIBUTORS

Jane N. Erin
Functional Vision Assessment

Robert L. Gordon
Low Vision Optometry

Diane L. Fazzi
Visual-Efficiency Training

Sherwin J. Isenberg
Pediatric Ophthalmology

Understanding the growth and development of the eye, developmental landmarks in vision, and the process of visual learning is essential when working with young visually impaired children and their families. A knowledge of the components of vision forms a basis for interpreting visual behaviors. Familiarity with the critical stages of visual development helps early-interventionists to plan appropriate visual-efficiency programming in order to ensure that young children function to their fullest potential.

Common causes of visual impairment in young children will be reviewed in this chapter. The roles of the pediatric ophthalmologist, the optometrist specializing in low vision, and the educational vision specialist are identified, and common assessment and intervention procedures are detailed.

GROWTH AND DEVELOPMENT OF THE EYE

The eye is the most developed organ of the body at birth, and it develops more quickly than any other after birth. From birth to maturity, the body increases to 21 times its birth size; the eye increases to 3 times its birth size and almost fully completes its growth at 3 years. The diameter of the eye is 15 mm at birth and 24 mm in adulthood. Of the 9 mm growth in diameter, one-third occurs in the first year, and growth is totally completed by puberty. Corneal diameter is approximately 9 mm-10 mm at birth, although it is sometimes smaller in the premature infant. In the adult the diameter is 11.75 mm. Corneal diameter is an important diagnostic tool. A larger-than-normal corneal diameter may indicate glaucoma, while a smaller-than-normal diameter may indicate microphthalmia. Blood vessels from the optic nerve emerge at 13 weeks' gestation and spread into the retina around toward the front of the eye. By 8-9 months' gestation, the retina is fully developed as determined by ophthalmoscopy (the retina completes histological maturation growth at 3 years of age).

The sequence of eye development can help determine the age of a premature infant. Both the macula at the center of the retina and the existence of iris blood vessels that are present only in utero can be used as landmarks for this purpose. The degree of development indicates the infant's gestational age.

The speed of the growth and development of the eye limits the time during which medical interventions are effective for children who may have congenital visual anomalies. Early diagnosis and treatment are important for the prevention, remediation, and stabilization of vision loss in the young child. A full discussion of congenital visual impairments is presented in a following section.

DEVELOPMENTAL LANDMARKS IN VISION

During the 12th week of gestation, the eyeballs form in the fetus. At birth, visual acuities are 20/200, at 1 year 20/50, and at 2 years, 20/20. That is, at birth the infant can see at 20 feet what someone with unimpaired sight can see at 200 feet, at 1 year can see at 20 feet what someone with unimpaired sight can see at 50 feet, and at 2 years has "normal" vision. Infants are born moderately farsighted and with astigmatism. By 1 year of age there is mild farsightedness, and approximately 8 percent of children have astigmatism. Accommodation, the change in the shape of the lens to adjust to looking at objects from different distances, is present at birth, and by 3-6 months it is adultlike in performance. Fixation, the ability to maintain a gaze on a light source or an object, becomes obvious at 6-8 weeks and is accurate by 6 months. Visual searching, which begins at 3 months, in combination with the development of fine motor abilities, forms the basis of eye-hand coordination. The ability to transfer objects from hand to hand typically emerges between 6 and 7 months, and the pincer grasp is refined at 10 months. Visual-form perception emerges at 12 months, when the child is able to see images and pictures and relate them to the real world.

The largest investigation of visual development has been performed by the Gesell Institute. The sequence of visual behaviors in infants that was identified by Gesell (1949) is outlined in Table 1. These developmental components of vision are rough gauges by which vision professionals can determine a young child's general functioning. They are not intended to be used as strict standards for visual diagnosis.

VISION: A LEARNED PROCESS

The use of vision is a learned process from which emerge an understanding of what is seen, knowledge of the location of objects in the environment, and the development of

Table 1. The Development of Visual Skills, by Sequence

Age of Onset of Behavior or Skill	Visual Behavior or Skill in the Infant
1 month	Follows objects with the eyes; blinks at a camera flash; moves head and eyes simultaneously in the same direction.
3 months	Reacts as if recognizes faces but actually reacts to voice and motion; has beginning visual attention.
5-6 months	Reaches for and grasps visual target; looks at distant targets.
7 months	Discriminates simple geometric patterns.
9 months	Perceives spatial relations with three dimensions.
12 months	Eye-hand coordination improves; able to shift gaze from far to near; tracks across 180-degree arc; uses eyes and hands together.
14 months	Shows visual interest in pictures; may point to pictures.
15 months	Follows moving objects well with the eyes; watches toys drop to the floor.
18 months	Develops spatial world similar to that of an adult.
24 months	Visually inspects objects without touching them.
48 months	Has fully developed visual system.

necessary reactions to visual stimuli. Vision involves all the body's parts and senses and requires the integration of all sensory information.

It is important to intervene early in the development of a visually impaired infant to provide the building blocks for as efficient and complete a visual system as possible. Corrective medical procedures that could improve vision, such as cataract or glaucoma surgery, need to occur within the first 2 months of life in order to allow the brain to process visual input accurately. Visual acuity must be developed during these first 6-8 weeks. If, for instance, cataract surgery is done beyond this critical period, the cataract may successfully be removed, but the child's visual acuity may not be improved beyond 20/200 due to immature visual processing. Human beings are, however, very adaptable. Young children will develop compensations for vision loss (they may tilt the head if necessary for clear vision, shift attention from one eye to the other, or suppress information from one eye in order to assist the brain in processing information from the other). Understanding the components of vision and the sequence of visual learning helps in the formulation of appropriate programming to increase visual efficiency for the young child.

COMPONENTS OF VISION

According to Corn's (1983) model of visual functioning (see Figure 1), the components of vision include visual abilities, stored and available individuality, and environmental cues. *Visual abilities* are often assessed by an ophthalmologist and include acuities, fields, ocular motility, brain functions, and light and color perception. The implications of *stored and available individuality* are reflected in the fact that two children with identical diagnoses and acuities may function differently. Among the factors accounting for these individual differences are the following:

- Cognition level,
- Sensory integration and development (the integration of visual input with other sensory systems),
- Perception,
- Psychological makeup, and
- Physical abilities.

Finally, *environmental cues* include characteristics of one's surroundings that provide information about the environment. Cues include the following:

- *Color*, which involves hue, brightness, and saturation,
- *Contrast*, which involves intensity in tone and color,
- *Time*, which involves the need to anticipate events, plan motor activities, and make long-term decisions,
- *Space*, which involves pattern, position, complexity, and clutter of visual stimuli, and
- *Illumination*, which involves aspects of lighting, such as intensity, location on the spectrum, reflective qualities, and distance of light sources.

All these factors can be varied to determine how a child functions visually under different conditions and to determine optimal environmental conditions for an individual child.

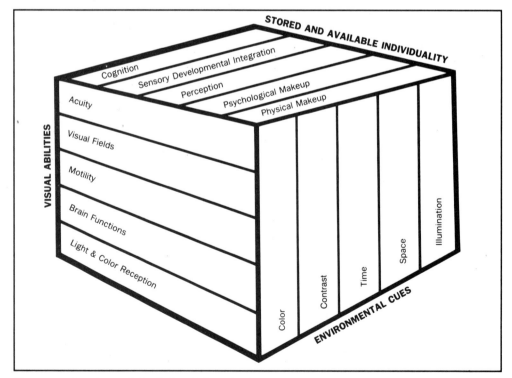

Figure 1. Corn's model of visual functioning. SOURCE: "Visual function: A model for individuals with low vision," *Journal of Visual Impairment & Blindness, 77* (8), p. 374.

SEQUENCE OF VISUAL LEARNING

Children normally develop many visual abilities. It is important to become familiar with those abilities and to use them in setting goals for the individual. The older and more severely impaired a student, the more important it is to be concerned with developmental sequence rather than adhering to developmental charts established according to chronological age. Such charts may not take into account general developmental delays. The development of vision occurs in the following sequences (Ferrell, 1985):

- First awareness, then attention, then understanding of stimuli,
- First attention to light, then to people, then to objects,
- First fixation, then tracking (visually following a moving object or light),
- First interest in near objects, then interest in distant objects,
- First peripheral (i.e., side) vision, then central vision,
- First preference for familiar stimuli, then preference for the novel,
- First viewing part of an object, then viewing a whole object,
- First interest in simple items, then interest in complex items and designs, and
- First interest in large items, then interest in small items.

Familiarity with the developmental sequence should form part of the knowledge base needed for intervention. For example, in designing an intervention strategy for a child who developmentally is unable to attend visually to his or her caretaker's face, it would be useless to spend large amounts of time trying to get the child to attend to a teddy bear because as a visual task, the latter would be developmentally more difficult for the child. Understanding the sequence of visual development can contribute to the creation of a well-designed environment and effective intervention for the young child with visual impairments.

CAUSES OF VISUAL IMPAIRMENT IN YOUNG CHILDREN

In order of decreasing frequency, the most common causes of visual impairment in children in the United States are prenatal cataracts; optic-nerve hypoplasia; retinopathy of prematurity (ROP); anophthalmia, microphthalmia, and glaucoma (which occur at the same frequency); and retinoblastoma. Less-frequently-occurring etiologies include myopia, albinism, and nystagmus.

The following section provides a brief discussion of some of the more common early childhood eye diseases and conditions. More thorough information can be found in a childhood ophthalmology text (such as those cited in the resource section at the end of this book) or obtained from a medical or vision specialist.

Acquired Eye Conditions

Pediatric eye conditions are categorized as acquired or congenital. Acquired conditions include ROP and a variety of conditions caused by trauma before or during birth or by infection.

Trauma. Trauma may be incurred by amniocentesis (rarely) or by forceps delivery. Symptoms—which generally decrease with time—include corneal edema (clouding or opacity), corneal striae (parallel lines), and retinal hemorrhage. Trauma, such as that resulting in hemorrhaging deep in the eye, may also be caused by abuse. Maternal drug intoxication is another cause of trauma. Cocaine addiction, for instance, causes possible infant addiction as well as thickness and irregularity of the blood vessels of the iris. Clinical impressions include visual inattentiveness; abnormal results of a visual-evoked response (VER) test (a computerized recording of electrical activity at the back of the brain which is used to assess problems in the retina-to-brain nerve pathway) in very young cocaine-exposed infants, with some improvement over time; a tendency toward delayed visual maturation; higher incidence of strabismus, a deviation in the position of one or both eyes; and refractive errors, which occur when light rays do not come to a point of focus on the retina and seem to respond well to corrective lenses. Cocaine and other drug intoxications can be treated with antagonists to the specific drug.

Infection. Several infections may affect the neonate. An inflammatory infection, ophthalmia neonatorum, is caused by bacteria and other organisms present in the birth canal, such as gonorrhea and chlamydia. Toxoplasmosis, a parasite acquired from beef and lamb, is passed from mother to child during birth and can cause scarring in the retina, nystagmus, and swelling of the brain with necrosis of the optic nerve. Systemic infections that may lead to visual impairment include herpes, cytomegalovirus, and rubella.

Infections may also be caused by the wearing of contact lenses, which are more frequently being prescribed for infants, especially following the removal of congenital cataracts. Sometimes tear proteins build up on the front surface of the contact lens, causing a reaction (called giant papillary conjunctivitis) in the conjunctival tissue lining the upper eyelid. This development presents a problem because the immediate treatment for the condition is removal of the contact lens, and without the lens the infant's vision is reduced. To avoid complete removal of the contact lenses, it is often possible to change the pattern of lens wearing (for example, four hours in one eye, four hours in the other).

Retinopathy of Prematurity. Premature babies born with a birthweight of less than 4 pounds (1,600 grams or less) or who are exposed to oxygen for 50 days or more are at significant risk of developing ROP. ROP is a retinal disorder that causes changes in the retinal blood vessels, and in some cases proliferation of the retinal blood vessels into the vitreous, the transparent gel-like substance at the back of the lens and eye that maintains the eye's shape. Fibrous tissues also develop through the retina and vitreous. The abundance of blood vessels and fibrous tissues cause stretching in the retina, which may lead to eventual detachment from the pigment epithelium, the outermost layer of the retina. Not all children with ROP are blind, but about 2,100 infants annually experience severe loss of vision from ROP in the United States, with the number rising as increasing numbers of smaller premature infants are surviving due to sophisticated neonatal technology (Trief, Duckman, Morse, & Silberman, 1989). Approximately 23 percent of these premature infants experience severe visual impairment or blindness from ROP. The international classification for ROP follows (Trief, Duckman, Morse, & Silberman, 1989).

- *Grade I.* Blood vessels grow to a defined line in the retina, so part of the retina is supplied with blood and part is not.
- *Grade II.* The line at which blood vessel growth stops becomes a ridge extending into the vitreous.
- *Grade III.* New blood vessels form in the ridge and may damage the retina.
- *Grade IV.* Fluid collects under the retina, and the retina is pulled out from its normal position in the back of the eye by the ridge (partial detachment).
- *Grade V.* Complete retinal detachment.

In many cases, the retinopathy will regress on its own, but 5 to 8 percent of infants with birthweights of under 2 pounds (1 kilogram) experience severe vision loss. ROP that does not regress on its own may be treated by a variety of methods, but no one effective method of prevention or treatment has yet been found. The most common treatments used are vitamin E therapy, photocoagulation, and cryotherapy surgery for retinal detachment. Research has produced mixed results on the effectiveness of these treatments.

Congenital Eye Conditions

Congenital anomalies encompass a wide variety of conditions, ranging from albinism to retinitis pigmentosa.

Albinism. Ocular albinism is a condition that allows light to pass through the iris, causing photophobia (light sensitivity). It is a hereditary deficiency in the pigment of the retina, iris, and choroid. In addition to being generally associated with photophobia, albinism is also associated with nystagmus and lack of depth perception. The use of sunwear to shield the eyes from glare and sunscreen to protect the skin is important for the young child with albinism.

Amblyopia. Amblyopia is also called lazy eye. It results in poor vision caused by the suppressed use of the eye rather than organic disease. Some loss of depth perception and visual field results, and blindness in one eye may occur if the condition is not treated. Deprivation amblyopia occurs in the newborn when normal vision in one eye is obstructed by a cataract, glaucoma, or other cause. Amblyopia can also result from strabismus (misalignment of the eyes), unequal refractive error (for example, one eye may be more nearsighted or have more astigmatism than the other), or other causes. Treatment for deprivation amblyopia is most effective in the first few months after birth. Amblyopia resulting from other causes may be responsive to treatment up to 9 years of age.

Aniridia. In aniridia, the iris does not form, creating light-control problems. Aniridia can be associated with kidney tumors and cataracts.

Anophthalmia. Anophthalmia is the absence of the globe (true eyeball), usually occurring in both eyes. Eyelids and lashes are present but may be closed or partially fused. The eyelid may appear sunken because of the absence of the globe.

Cataracts. Congenital cataracts are a clouding of the lens that causes reduced visual acuity and increased glare due to the scattering of light in the eye. They are caused by rubella or galactosemia (a hereditary metabolic disorder in which an infant is unable to convert the galactose in milk into blood sugar, causing galactose to diffuse into the lens), or they may be of familial origin. Cataracts are treated surgically by lensectomy, or the removal of the clouded lens, followed by optical correction. If they are not treated early, the child may develop nystagmus and amblyopia.

Coloboma. A coloboma is a congenital cleft due to the failure of some portion of the eye to complete growth during development. The pupil may have a teardrop shape, which may cause difficulty with glare. Contact lenses and sunglasses are used to effect cosmetic improvement and reduce photophobia.

Cortical Visual Impairment. Children with cortical visual impairment appear to have intact visual systems and normal pupillary response. Vision loss is caused by damage to the visual cortex of the brain. Visual abilities may improve with visual-efficiency training, with peripheral vision increasing first. Incorporating tactile and kinesthetic modalities in visual-efficiency training may enhance vision use in the child with cortical visual impairment.

Glaucoma. Glaucoma, or increased pressure in the eye, causes a clouding of vision and can lead to loss of peripheral vision and eventual blindness if untreated. Symptoms of glaucoma include a large cornea, redness, pain, or frequent rubbing of the eyes, as well as excessive tearing. In some cases, however, there may be no symptoms at all. Early detection is important and treatment with drops, laser therapy, or surgery may be recommended.

Microphthalmia. Microphthalmia is a condition marked by abnormally small eyes. It can occur with colobomas and is often associated with defects of the skull, vitreous anomalies, glaucoma, and cataracts.

Myopia. Myopia is a technical term for nearsightedness characterized by clear near vision and blurred distance vision. It can often be corrected with lenses.

Nystagmus. Nystagmus is characterized by an involuntary, rhythmical oscillating movement of one or both eyes from side to side, up and down, in a rotary pattern, or in some combination. Nystagmus may accompany other eye conditions or may exist alone. Some children may turn or tilt their heads as they try to control the eye movements to improve focusing.

Optic-Nerve Hypoplasia. Optic-nerve hypoplasia is manifested in the form of an underdeveloped optic nerve in one or both eyes. Vision loss varies from moderate to severe. Poor growth due to hormonal defects may be associated with this condition.

Peter's Anomaly. Peter's anomaly is a rare congenital ocular malformation in which the cornea may be scarred, and cataracts and glaucoma may be present due to failure or delay in the separation of the lens of the eye from the epithelium.

Retinitis Pigmentosa. Retinitis pigmentosa, a hereditary condition that progressively affects peripheral and night vision and can lead to tunnel vision or blindness, can be diagnosed in young children. However, the symptoms rarely manifest themselves to a significant degree until later childhood.

All of the childhood eye conditions identified in the previous section can be treated or addressed, as appropriate, by a variety of specialists with expertise in the area of visual impairment. The specialists include, but are not limited to, the pediatric ophthalmologist, the optometrist specializing in low vision, and the vision specialist. The pediatric ophthalmologist is a medical doctor (M.D.) who diagnoses and treats eye diseases in children, performs surgery, and prescribes other types of treatment, including eyeglasses, other optical devices, or drugs, when necessary. The optometrist specializing in low vision is a licensed, nonmedical specialist (O.D.) trained to work with the functioning rather than the pathology of the eye. This specialist measures refraction and prescribes and fits corrective lenses and low vision devices. The vision specialist is a teacher of visually impaired students or orientation and mobility (O&M) instructor with specialized expertise in working with visually impaired children in areas such as functional vision assessments and training, optical device training, and integration of visual functioning into daily routines at school, home, or in the community. All of these specialists contribute to the growth and development of the child with a visual impairment.

ROLE OF THE PEDIATRIC OPHTHALMOLOGIST

Pediatric ophthalmologists are specifically oriented toward early diagnosis and treatment of eye disease in children. They are concerned with the following areas:

- Congenital anomalies,
- Normal eye development,
- Refractive errors,
- Strabismus,
- Amblyopia, and
- Reading problems.

Although the ophthalmologist not specializing in pediatrics may address the same concerns, he or she may not be oriented toward early intervention and may not be trained in the prevention of chronic conditions.

The following techniques and areas are addressed during an examination by a pediatric ophthalmologist:

- Assessment of visual acuity by a variety of techniques, such as the use of a nystagmus drum to induce nystagmus visually.
- Use of targets such as finger puppets, which encourage the child to follow visually; the quality of eye movement as well as the ability to do the task are assessed.
- Examination of the front of the eye using a penlight, portable biomicroscope, and, if indicated, a tonometer to measure pressure within the eye.
- Examination of the back of the eye, which is especially important when ROP is suspected.

Parents of young children can help the ophthalmologist in several ways. Providing access to previous eye examination reports, evaluations of the child's functional vision, old photographs for visual comparison of eye appearance, and any eyeglasses or optical devices the child uses will be helpful to the examining physician. In addition, it is important to inform the ophthalmologist about any medications the child is using. Communication between the parents and the pediatric ophthalmologist is an important element in the effective treatment of the visually impaired infant.

A nystagmus drum may be used to help assess visual acuity.

ROLE OF THE OPTOMETRIST SPECIALIZING IN LOW VISION

Optometrists working with young visually impaired children who have some degree of visual functioning should have specialized training and experience in the area of low vision (impaired vision that is good enough to be used as a major channel for learning). It is also helpful if they have had experience working with young children. Optometrists may address refractive errors, visual efficiency, prescription of eyeglasses and contact lenses, and prescription of optical devices.

The optometrist takes a variety of factors into account when performing a low vision assessment. He or she is interested in the child's history of functional vision and so works closely with the child's parents and teacher of visually impaired students to determine their perceptions of the child's problems. Informal observation of the child's use of vision includes such areas as these:

● Appearance of the eye,
● The child's approach to investigating new objects,
● Presence of compensations such as head tilt, head turn, or squinting, and
● The child's reaction to light and changes in lighting.

Other abilities, skills, and factors the optometrist addresses are the following:

● Awareness of surroundings and visual stimuli,

- Muscle balance,
- Eye preference (if the preferred, or better, eye is covered, the child will usually protest vigorously),
- Shape of the cornea,
- Presence of refractive error (i.e., examination for near- and farsightedness and astigmatism),
- Possibility of inducing nystagmus with an optokinetic nystagmus drum,
- Fixation abilities,
- Tracking, or the ability to follow a moving target,
- Binocular vision, or the use of two eyes together in a rapid, concise, and spontaneous pattern,
- Convergence,
- Stereopsis and depth perception, which is the determination of relative distance in space, using clues such as apparent size, density of color, and perspective,
- Field of vision, or the area over which vision is possible (ability to detect motion, awareness of objects, and night vision are encompassed within this factor), and
- Form perception, or the ability to organize and recognize visual sensations as shapes.

Visual acuities are also determined. There are many ways to test visual acuities, such as by using Tumbling E charts (charts displaying Es of different sizes facing different directions), object-silhouette targets (such as shapes of houses and umbrellas), and hand-position cards (charts with diagrams of hands facing different directions). However, these tests require a response that the very young child may not be able to provide. A VER test may be used to help determine acuities when the child is unable to respond motorically. This test measures the brain's response to light and pattern stimulation.

In very young infants, the optometrist checks that the eyes move together, that there is a full range of eye movement, and that no large refractive errors are present. Frequently, the assessment is carried out over several visits.

Low vision devices may be prescribed for the child by the optometrist. These devices include magnifiers for near tasks, closed-circuit televisions for viewing pictures and letters, tinted lenses for light-control problems, and telescopes for distance tasks. Low vision devices may be provided in addition to any refractive corrections that can be made.

When working with infants and preschoolers, it is important for the optometrist to maintain contact with the variety of professionals and family members involved with the child. This teamwork helps to ensure an effective program for the child and family. Typically, children with some degree of usable vision would benefit from examination by or consultation with an ophthalmologist, optometrist, and vision specialist to determine which treatments and disciplines are needed.

ROLE OF THE VISION SPECIALIST

The vision specialist, who may be a credentialed teacher of the visually impaired or an orientation and mobility (O&M) specialist, is primarily concerned with:

- Functional vision assessment,
- Visual-efficiency training,
- Optical device training,
- Integration of visual functioning into daily routines, and
- Coordination of all participants of the vision team, including eye care specialists and family members.

Functional Vision Assessment

A functional vision assessment determines how much usable vision a child has to perform visual tasks. The resulting report should include the following:

- A summarization of medical reports;
- Observations of near and distance vision, visual field, and ocular motility as used in regular daily activity;
- Description of procedures and activities used in assessment;
- Statement of eligibility for vision services, based on visual functioning; and
- Recommendations.

Formal vs. Informal Procedures. The functional vision assessment is an informal procedure. Formalized procedures are often inappropriate for the very young or severely disabled child because many require responses that these children are unable to produce. In addition, standard devices may not be appropriate for this population because of the variety of factors affecting the child's visual functioning. These factors include

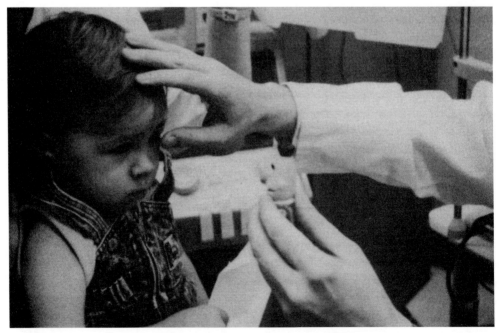

Objects that hold interest for a child and prompt the child's attention can be used during the assessment of the child's visual functioning.

medications that affect vision or state of consciousness, the child's limited attention span, and possible decreased activity level.

Screenings. Screenings can be used to support the functional vision assessment and to help determine a child's need for ongoing service. Screenings commonly used are the Infant Vision Checklist and the Peabody Functional Vision Inventory for Multiply and Severely Handicapped Children.

The Infant Vision Checklist (Vision Screening Project, 1980) covers a wide variety of areas including:

- Pupillary responses,
- The Hirschberg corneal reflex test, consisting of holding a light 12 in. from the eyes and looking for the reflection—if the eyes are aligned, the reflections are balanced,
- Momentary regard of objects,
- Momentary regard of a person,
- Prolonged regard of objects,
- Horizontal eye coordination,
- Ability to follow a moving person visually,
- Vertical and circular eye coordination,
- Free inspection of surroundings,
- Ability to turn the eyes to light and objects,
- Ability to follow an object from central to peripheral areas,
- Tendency to blink at the shadow of a hand,
- Ability to follow a ball left to right visually,
- Tendency to reach for objects (not the same as grasp),
- The cover test, used to detect strabismus and amblyopia, in which vision in one eye is occluded and the occluder is then quickly moved to the other eye—when the "good" eye is occluded, the amblyopic eye will align, and
- The two-light test for peripheral-field assessment, in which one light acts as a distracter while the other is moved to various points and the ability to shift gaze from center to peripheral points is observed.

The Peabody Inventory (Langley, 1980) includes both a screening inventory and a functional vision inventory. Some of the items are similar to those of the Infant Vision Checklist, addressing such areas as:

- Pupillary responses,
- Tendency to blink at the shadow of a hand,
- Ability to orient peripherally,
- Tendency to fixate on 4-in. objects,
- Shifting gaze,
- Tendency to reach in response to a visual cue,
- Ability to track horizontally, vertically, and circularly,
- Convergence, or the ability to follow an object as it approaches (the child's eyes

should demonstrate esotropia [the eye turning inward] at about 4 in.; with a muscle imbalance there may be early convergence of one eye), and

- Ability to track or pick up a small object; tested with 3 mm and 1 mm beads and thread by scattering larger beads first, then the smaller and the thread, and having the child locate each.

Screenings for acuity are generally designed for students functioning at the 2-year level or above. Two screening devices that may be used with very young children are Lighthouse Acuity Cards and the Parson's Visual Acuity Test.

Lighthouse Cards (1980) have several advantages for use with young children:

- Distracters are written on cards separate from the stimulus cards.
- The cards are based on three basic symbols (house, umbrella, apple) and require only consistent (rather than accurate) labeling; for example, a child may call the umbrella a mushroom, as long as it is always identified as a mushroom throughout the test.
- The cards are plastic and so easily cleaned.

The Parson's Visual Acuity Test (1979) was developed for severely disabled individuals and may be used with children from 18 months; the test does not depend on language for results, and a training component is included with the test. The Parson's test provides acuities only.

Assessment. After screening is completed, assessment is carried out. Langley's (1980) materials, available from the Stoelting Company in Chicago, can be used for both screening and assessment. The materials are extensive, and activities for vision usage are provided. Some items included in the assessment, resulting in a vision profile, are:

- Observation of eye structure,
- The noting of behaviors incompatible with vision, such as hand flapping, eye poking, and the like.
- Observation of the use of eyeglasses (for example, looking over or under the lenses, or otherwise avoiding their use),
- Observation of the ability to deal with obstacles (difficulty descending stairs is noted, as is balking at stairs),
- Observation of reflexive and voluntary eye movements,
- Observation of near and distance vision (for instance, the distance at which the child will search for an item is noted, as is the size of the item),
- Observation of the ability to locate dropped objects (the child must have developed object permanence [the understanding that objects exist even when they cannot be seen] to do this),
- Observation of the ability to match pictures,
- Estimations of acuity,
- Testing for field assessment, and
- Assessment of visual perceptual skills.

Functional Vision Kit. Materials for functional vision assessment are not standardized. It is important to include items that will be motivating for the child. Some suggestions for basic materials to include in a kit are occluders, measuring tape, penlights, colored light bulbs, an extension cord, Styrofoam balls, balloons, matching cards, cause-and-effect toys, lighted toys, sounded toys, reflective toys, foil balls, rolling toys, bubble-making toys, pom-poms, and scarves.

It may be helpful to package items according to size for easy reference. It also may be helpful to include stickers for marking specific distances in a room (5 ft., 10 ft., and so on).

When working with an individual child, it may help to make a list of all materials with which the child has regular contact and use these items to start. Next, making a list of those items that may be unfamiliar but that seem to be motivating to the child and noting their common characteristics may be useful. On the basis of these listings, it is possible to construct a set of materials that incorporates the characteristics of the preferred materials with those of the unfamiliar items.

The most difficult aspect of assessing functional vision is deciding whether a child's lack of response is due to an inability to see, to a lack of motivation to see, or to an inability to respond. Care should be taken when assessing functional vision to use objects with no auditory clues, to ensure that the child is truly responding visually and not just reacting to the sound stimuli. It is important to be aware that motivations can vary and not to make assumptions regarding the child's motivation. In terms of planning materials and programming, it is essential to be aware of both motivation and function.

These sample items from a functional vision kit include toys and other objects children find visually stimulating.

Visual-Efficiency Training

Visual-efficiency training, or the process of learning to use vision, involves two functions: understanding visual information and coordinating motor activity with vision. The goal of using visual-efficiency activities with young children is to move from a level of awareness of the visual stimuli to a level of understanding of what the stimuli mean and coordinating vision with other actions. Children with multiple disabilities often experience the added challenge of increased difficulty in responding physically to visual stimuli, and cognitive delays often serve to decrease the motivation to use what visual abilities they possess. Visual-efficiency training is a most appropriate intervention for this population as well.

Visual-efficiency training may be approached from two different perspectives, developmental or functional. In the developmental approach, visual skills are taught and reinforced according to appropriate developmental sequences of vision usage (for example, working on visual fixation with the goal of working up to visual tracking in the future). In the functional approach, visual behaviors are practiced and learned through functional tasks that may occur naturally during the process of a normal day (for example, working on both fixation and tracking during mealtime).

Developmental visual-efficiency training activities may include tracking a penlight, scanning a wall to locate a given picture, using puzzles to expand visual memory skills, and practicing figure-ground recognition with commercially available line drawings and photos. There are many creative varieties of developmental activities that most commonly utilize simulated materials and environments to promote visual efficiency. Although artificial means are used in the efficiency training, the ultimate goal is for the visually impaired child to develop and utilize visual abilities to the fullest potential in daily life.

Functional visual-efficiency training activities may include spotting the bar of soap at the edge of the bath during bathtime, scanning the pantry to locate a box of cereal, tracking a spoon full of food in order to open one's mouth at the appropriate time, and fixating on a mother's face during breast-feeding. Functional activities have endless possibilities, as they promote visual efficiency through encouraging the child to participate in activities that require the use of vision. Through these experiences the child begins to learn the natural consequences of using vision.

Developmental and functional approaches to visual-efficiency training are not mutually exclusive. Appropriate strategy determinations need to be made for individual children for specific skills. Different approaches may prove to be more beneficial for various situations at various times. Developmental and functional approaches may actually complement one another when they are applied in a sensitive, individualized manner.

When professionals and parents are working on visual-efficiency tasks, it is important that no value judgments be expressed in response to the child's visual functioning. It is easy to communicate subtly that it is "better" if the child sees more. Many times the child is using vision to the best of his or her ability, and a child's self-esteem should never be tied to praise for visual performance. Families and professionals may encourage the young visually impaired child to "tell me what you see on the shelf" or

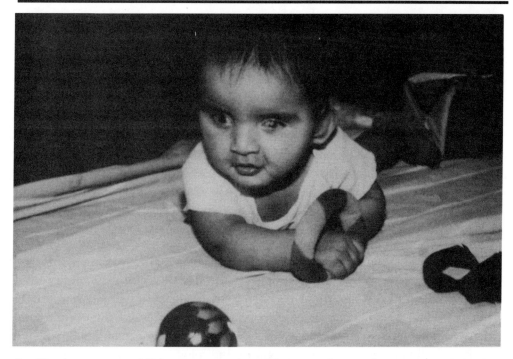

Positioning a young child near motivating objects can be used to promote behaviors like lifting the head, reaching, and visual scanning.

"describe what the doll looks like." By accepting the response and moving on from there, adults encourage the use of vision as well as honest responses. Vision simply *is*, and while it is beneficial to encourage children to use their vision to the greatest degree possible, phrases of praise should be used with caution in visual-efficiency training.

Visual efficiency may be optimized when auditory, tactile, kinesthetic, and motor-skill components are integrated into the training process. Multisensory experiences provide the most accurate and complete input for the young visually impaired or multiply impaired child. For example, a child who sees a jack-in-the-box will understand the concept more fully if he or she is able to touch and activate the toy and listen to the many sounds it makes. This involvement provides the young child with the necessary verification to assist in the development of needed concepts and may also motivate the visually impaired child to investigate places and objects within the environment, thus encouraging further use of vision.

The ultimate goal of visual-efficiency training is to coordinate the purposeful use of vision with activity. Integrating other sensory modalities into the training process is key in promoting this development. For example, encouraging young children to look and listen to events in the surrounding environment (for example, watching Mom wash dishes while listening to the running water and clinking dishes), allowing children to touch objects that they may usually only see from a distance (for example, exploring the gas pump and nozzle that may be seen from the car), and requiring children to engage in visual tasks while moving or being moved (for example, crawling in pursuit of a moving wind-up toy) are methods that incorporate multiple sensory systems in visual-efficiency development. These same methods would be similarly appropriate for interventions with multiply impaired children with low vision, although more physical assistance may be needed. Sensory integration should begin with infant-parent interactions (such as stroking the child's face before breast-feeding, gentle rocking in conjunction with mother's soft singing, and encouraging the child to look at the caregiver's face during cuddling and playing) in order to promote improved eye contact and more positive interactions. The social skill of good eye contact, when developed early, can prove to be beneficial throughout the visually impaired child's life. Feeding, whether breast-, bottle-, or spoon-feeding, is another early incentive for visual-efficiency training that involves many visual skills and high levels of motivation. Parents can have a vital role in reinforcing their child's visual-efficiency skills during daily routines. Young children with low vision need abundant opportunities and continual encouragement to utilize their sensory abilities and eventually to become comfortable and competent in doing so.

Environmental Considerations for Enhancing the Use of Vision

The environment is an important part of visual-efficiency training. According to Corn's model of visual functioning (1983), (see Figure 1), environmental cues to consider when designing a stimulating environment for the young child with low vision may include illumination, space, time, contrast, and color.

Illumination. Proper illumination can increase the visibility of objects, tasks, and activities within the child's environment. The intensity of the light may be increased or decreased according to the individual child's functioning. As a general rule, children with optic atrophy, macular degeneration, and retinitis pigmentosa tend to function better with increased illumination, while children with particular types of cataracts, aniridia, and albinism seem to function best under minimal-intensity lighting. These general rules provide only a starting point and should not be adhered to rigidly. Needs for illumination are highly individualized, and all options should be explored before determinations are made.

Glare is a constant consideration for all individuals with low vision. When selecting positioning for the young child or for portable lighting sources, avoid creating shadows and avoid reflecting the light directly into the child's eyes. Minimize glare whenever possible. Be sensitive to changing lighting conditions outdoors. Visors and specially made sunglasses for children will help to eliminate some of the glare experienced outdoors.

Space. For the person with low vision, space is an important visual organizer. Simple patterns are more easily viewed than complex ones. Objects placed too close together may be difficult for the young visually impaired child to distinguish properly from one another. These considerations are relevant when making room-decorating decisions and when arranging toys or eating implements for the child. Allow adequate space between items to avoid visual clutter and overwhelming sensory input for the child with limited vision.

Time. Individuals with visual impairments often require additional time to complete tasks that require the use of vision. Young children may interpret sensory input at a slower rate. Activities that require a degree of anticipation (such as play with switch-activated toys and jack-in-the-boxes) may initially be difficult for a child who is being asked to retain visual information. Young visually impaired children should be allowed extra time to complete visual tasks. If toys whose use heavily involves a time element seem unable to hold a child's interest, try toys that prompt more immediate interplay until the child develops stronger visual retention abilities.

Contrast. Maximizing contrast between objects and work surfaces can help children with low vision maintain a greater sense of control over the items that they manipulate. Higher-contrast items are easier to locate, distinguish, and keep track of. Cookie sheets with white contact paper on one side and dark on the other make playing with small items easier for the visually impaired child. Contrasting place mats on the table-top help children to define their eating space and to locate their food more efficiently. Placing a light-colored bath soap in a dark-colored soap dish makes it easier for the young child to find and begin to assume a degree of independence during bathtime. Wherever possible in the home and at school, contrast should be maximized to facilitate greater independence and increased use of vision.

Color. Color selection is an important environmental consideration. Infants prefer to look at black-and-white geometric patterns, with lines being approximately 3/4 in. in width. Primary colors are more quickly seen by the older child, with red attracting the most attention. Color preference and visibility are highly individualized and must be explored with the young visually impaired child to determine which colors are easiest for the child to distinguish.

Making environmental modifications in the home and at school may encourage environmental exploration, independence, and functional use of vision in the young visually impaired child. Facilitating increased participation in activities of daily living, preacademics, recreation, and socialization through environmental sensitivity can help the young child to acquire positive, enriching experiences that may form the basis for future life successes.

Young children with visual impairments function at varied levels and have varied prognoses for visual development. Understanding the medical and functional implications of visual impairment helps the professional plan intervention strategies. Vision care specialists, teachers of the visually impaired, O&M specialists, and family members need to work together to formulate an accurate picture of the young child's visual functioning. As a team, families and professionals can develop and implement an individualized plan that will minimize the frustrations associated with vision loss and maximize the successes associated with increased visual efficiency.

Chapter 3

COGNITIVE FOCUS: DEVELOPING COGNITION, CONCEPTS, AND LANGUAGE IN YOUNG BLIND AND VISUALLY IMPAIRED CHILDREN

CONTRIBUTORS

Karen M. Finello
Cognitive Development

Nancy Hedlund Hanson
*Concept, Tactile, and Auditory
    Development*

Linda S. Kekelis
Language Development

Vision is the primary system of sensory input for human beings; it is the basis for the majority of human learning. When it is reduced or eliminated, there is a major impact on the individual as a whole. When vision loss occurs during early childhood, the development of cognition, concepts, and language is altered during sensitive stages of the child's development. In order to compensate for lack of vision, it is important for the visually impaired child to maintain activity in and involvement with the environment. All too often, passivity becomes the most disabling aspect of blindness in children.

Vision is a key motivator for activity, for it provides consistent information about the environment and immediate feedback for and verification of other sensory experiences. The visual sense presents the world to the young child in an integrated form. Vision is also a distance sense, that is, it provides the child with information about objects outside the nearby environment. Without vision, an individual must rely on verbal descriptions or self-exploration to learn about the world. Verbal descriptions provide information from another person's perspective and are often incomplete. Self-exploration is limited in the amount of information that can be accessible to the young child without vision. Many things are simply too large, too small, too fragile, or too abstract for the child to explore tactilely or auditorily. Therefore, blind children do not have the benefit of rapidly and completely perceiving objects and events in the environment. They need specialized instruction and strategies for learning about their world in order to compensate for their vision loss.

The need for appropriate concept development is especially critical for the blind child, who receives fragmented and inaccurate sensory input. It is primarily through tactile and auditory processing that the visually impaired child learns about the environment. This chapter highlights the effects of vision loss on the cognitive development of the young visually impaired child. Because language acquisition is an integral part of concept and cognitive development, the chapter identifies developmental sequences in the areas of cognition, concept formulation, and language, relating them to appropriate intervention strategies that may be implemented by families, early childhood educators, and specialized professionals.

IMPORTANCE OF VISION

Cognitive development involves the development of the thinking skills related to concepts, abstractions, and mental representations. Early measures of cognitive development reflect the progression of motor-skills sequences, which is as follows:

- From gross motor to fine motor,
- From head to toe,
- From proximal (parts of the body toward the trunk) to distal (parts of the body away from the trunk) locations, and
- From simple to complex.

Many motor skills are learned from imitation and visual stimulation to motivate the activity. In sighted children, vision becomes the lead modality by 3 months of age and the principal source of information about the environment by 6 months of age. A blind child must learn to use other sensory modalities for gathering environmental information. Audition is commonly considered the compensatory modality for individuals with vision loss. However, the auditory system develops more slowly than does the visual system, so the blind child has a slower developmental scale to follow for learning about the environment.

Making use of tactile input is another compensatory modality for children with vision loss, but tactile learning is different from visual learning. Tactile exploration takes longer than does visual exploration, and the learner often needs to feel an object repeatedly in order to obtain an accurate idea of what it is like. Minor details may be lost, especially in hasty or unsystematic explorations.

COGNITIVE DEVELOPMENT IN THE INFANT

For an infant, tactile sensation is primary. The tactile sense is key and operational at birth. Vision is not the primary channel for sensory input for the newborn infant because normally it is not well developed at birth. It is important to try to interact with the infant as close to the time of birth as possible because this is when the infant is most tactilely available and likely to be receptive to tactile input. Most sighted infants are receptive to touch and like to be covered and cuddled. However, many infants who are premature or ill at birth have not had only pleasant experiences with being touched. At best, intensive-care units and hospitals provide a mixture of pleasurable and painful experiences, and an infant who has been subject to a medical stay may consequently not enjoy the touch of a familiar adult or a soft toy. Without visual fore-warning, visually impaired infants may be startled by some tactile experiences.

Infants are most receptive to touch near the mouth, where sucking and eating take place. In general, infants are tuned into bodily feelings (hunger, sleepiness, wet dia-pers, and so on). Their systems are set up to respond to touch. It is important to help the visually impaired child progress from responding positively to touch to reaching out to receive tactile experiences. Tactile function follows a sequence that begins with engaging in hand-to-mouth play and progresses to reaching away from the body. The child should be encouraged to investigate the space near him- or herself, such as the crib or the caretaker's face. Once the child begins to investigate the immediate environ-ment, more active manipulation should be encouraged. For example, once the visually impaired child investigates a mobile hanging above the crib, the child should be assist-ed in pulling or batting the mobile. As cause-and-effect relationships between batting the mobile and hearing musical sounds are established, objects that extend beyond the infant's immediate reach can begin to act as motivators for the child to move.

Sequence of Hand Skills

Being able to grasp and manipulate objects helps the infant develop ideas about objects, actions, three-dimensional space, and causal relationships between events. Blind children typically do not follow the same developmental sequence of manual activity as sighted children do. (Table 1 outlines this sequence.) They may not demon-

Table 1. Usual Developmental Sequence for Hand Skills in Sighted Children

Age at Which Behavior Develops	Behavior Demonstrated
Birth	No manual control demonstrated.
1 week	Forearm, hand, and fingers act as one.
1 month	Child stares at a suspended object but does not reach for it.
2 months	Child clenches fingers to palm, may hold an object for a short time, then drops the object.
3 months	Child swipes at dangling objects with fist.
4 months	Child shows interest in fingers and midline placement of hands (in the middle of the body or near the mouth).
4-6 months	Child reaches, grasps, may bring an object to the mouth, and may begin to coordinate posture, vision, and arm-and-hand movements.
7 months	Grasp changes from palmar (squeeze grasp with no thumb involvement) to thumb with several fingers.
8 months	Ability to transfer an object from hand to hand.
9 months	Thumb approaches forefinger in an effort to grasp.

strate midline play at 4 months or reaching at 5 months. Visually impaired infants generally maintain fisted hands while at rest, with the fists positioned at shoulder height. The child with light perception but no form perception may begin to engage in certain mannerisms at about 5 months of age. These mannerisms, such as eye poking and finger flicking, serve to provide the visually impaired child with additional sensory input. The blind infant's world is often a sensory void in which things happen at random. The mouth remains the primary organ of perception until well into the second year of life. The hands give only limited information about the world, and while the child is at a young age, tactile exploration lacks a high degree of intentionality. Without appropriate intervention, there is a risk that the child's personality will remain centered in body sensations. The goal of intervention is to help the child bridge the distance between the self and the world outside the self. It is important, therefore, to try to redirect mannerisms and body-centered self-stimulation, which isolate the visually impaired child from the environment, toward outlets that involve meaningful environmental interactions. Mannerisms may be redirected by providing alternate forms of stimulation and by creating a safe environment that encourages the child's involvement. For further discussion of this topic, see Chapter 5.

Object Permanence

The concept of object permanence is the basic understanding that an object exists whether or not it is seen. This understanding progresses through four phases and is fully developed in the normally sighted infant at approximately 18 months of age; without appropriate planned intervention, blind children tend to lag in this area of development by approximately one year. The sequence of the development of object permanence is shown in Table 2.

Auditory cuing can assist the visually impaired child in developing an understanding of object permanence. For example, after placing her blind child in the crib, a child's mother may continue to talk to the child, making her presence in the room known. Older children should be encouraged to search the immediate area for an

Table 2. Sequence of Development of Object Permanence

Developmental Phase	Behavior Demonstrated
I	The child reaches for a partially hidden object if he or she has watched it being hidden.
II	The child searches for a completely hidden object if he or she has watched it being hidden; if the object is removed from the original spot, the child continues to search in the first place in which he or she saw it hidden.
III	A change in location does not affect the child's mental representation of an object (understanding of the idea or concept of an object); if the child watches an object being hidden and then moved, he or she searches in the place to which it has been moved.
IV	The child is able to use imagination to judge where a hidden object is located.

object that has been dropped. Too often it is easier for the adult to pick up or discard dropped items for the blind child. Assisting the child in locating dropped objects helps promote the development of object permanence and future concept development.

COGNITIVE DEVELOPMENT IN THE PRESCHOOLER

Concepts, Abstractions, and Classifications

During the preschool period, abstract thinking and the development of other complex concepts are typically observed. However, in blind children there is generally a substantial delay in the formation of an inner representational system that includes independent actions and behaviors of others. Blind children often gather information from people in an attempt to substitute it for information that they cannot obtain visually.

Concepts are formed by the organization of information into generalizations (for example, many children begin by identifying all four-legged animals as dogs until their generalizations contain more information), and abstractions capture the essence of the commonality among them. Visually impaired children's concepts are often based on different sets of information derived from nonvisual sources. For example, the blind child's concept of dog may be connected to initial tactile experiences (that is, dogs may be thought of as small, fluffy animals if the child's interaction has been with a spaniel). Classifications occur when groups of objects are defined on the basis of their similarities and excluded on the basis of their differences. Classifications by the blind child may be based on alternative sensory modalities that may lead the child to make inaccurate or limited categorizations.

Developing concepts, abstractions, and classifications involves critical cognitive skills for any child. Hence, blind children are at a developmental disadvantage because they must rely on senses other than vision to obtain information. It is therefore important to provide blind children with a great deal of hands-on experience and verbal information about the environment to help them compensate for the lack of visual information available to them.

Role of Play

Play is important in the development of concepts at the preschool level. Mental development may lead to increased curiosity and exploration, as a result of which children learn cause-and-effect relationships and develop new skills by combining parts of behaviors in different sequences in play. Through exploratory play, the young child develops the ability to use tools that are then used to solve problems.

Experiential deficits in blind children that are caused by limited mobility, diminished motivation, and overprotectiveness on the part of parents or caretakers contribute to lags in the development of symbolic play. Symbolic play is play in which symbols are used to represent objects in the play situation (for example, when children use sand and water as the ingredients for a pretend cake). If the child lacks opportunity for imitation, play remains concrete and manipulative—that is, physical actions are taken with an object in order to gain control of it (for example, when children close and wind up a jack-in-the box)—rather than progressing to more abstract forms. Blind children tend to engage in concrete, manipulative play more than symbolic play, but eventually manipulative play helps the child develop the ability to use representation in more situations.

Imitative Skills

Many skills are learned through imitation. The phases of imitation include:

- *Pseudoimitation*, in which the infant is capable of imitating only those actions that already exist in his or her repertoire.
- *True imitation*, in which the child imitates novel behavior, but only with body parts that he or she can see.
- *Imitation of new actions and those involving body parts the child cannot see*, in which the child may imitate facial expressions, tongue movements, and so on.
- *Deferred imitation*, in which the child imitates actions seen previously; this occurs at the same time object permanence develops.

For a blind child, the development of imitative skills may literally require feeling the movements of another person's body. It is important to provide a variety of tactile experiences with movement for the young blind child.

Conservation

Conservation is the understanding that mass remains constant when contents are transferred to different containers (for example, the amount of milk poured from one glass to another remains the same even though the size and shape of the glasses are different). The order of acquisition of the concepts involved in conservation is similar in sighted and blind children. (The order of acquisition of understanding is mass, weight, and then volume.) Sensory discrimination is often less sophisticated in younger children. Because of their sensory deprivation, blind children may have an understanding of conservation similar to that of sighted children younger than they are.

AUDITORY DEVELOPMENT

In order for a child to attend to sensory input, meaning must be assigned to it. Visually impaired children receive much auditory stimulation that is meaningless to them. Meaningless or overwhelming auditory stimuli are often tuned out. An auditory stimulus is meaningless when it cannot be connected to a familiar object or concept. For example, the noise of a vacuum cleaner is meaningless to a blind child who has never felt the machine or who does not relate its sound to a function that is understood.

Sound-related input differs from visual and tactile input in that the individual has little control over it. Interpreting auditory input requires a high degree of focus, and sound tends to be received passively by people.

Unlike vision, which begins at birth, auditory function begins before birth in the womb, where pleasant sounds may be associated with pleasant feelings. Despite its early development, the auditory system does not provide the integration afforded by the visual sense. Auditory function develops in the following sequence (Gleason, 1984):

- reflexive responses to auditory stimuli
- attention to auditory stimuli
- localization of auditory stimuli
- discrimination of sounds (the child analyzes and categorizes)
- recognition of auditory stimuli (the child obtains meaning and associates)
- comprehension of auditory stimuli (the child understands verbalizations).

Hearing without vision provides incomplete information. Sound can, however, motivate children to move, can reinforce their reaching, and can encourage them to keep trying.

The search for and recovery of objects on the basis of sound cues alone are late achievements of the blind infant, occurring during the last quarter of the first year. Auditory cues do not give substance to an object in the absence of vision because there is no information that unites the tactile experience of touching the object to the sound.

The ability to search for and recover objects on sound cues alone develops in the stages outlined in Table 3 (Davis & Langley, 1980). At approximately 11 months, both sighted and blind children use sound cues for cognitive purposes; they will search for and pick up sound-producing objects. The ability to react to a sound anticipates the ability to use sound as an indicator of the sound-producing object. Before a child can respond with direct reach on the basis of a sound cue alone, he or she must solve a conceptual problem. First, the child must determine that the sound signifies that something exists; second, the child needs to realize that the object has both tactile and acoustical properties constituting its identity and wholeness. (For example, before a blind child will search for a musical toy, the child must be able to associate the auditory music with the tactile toy. He or she needs to have formed a complete concept of the musical toy and to be motivated to search for it).

By 2 years of age, blind children who find an adaptive solution to this conceptual problem can localize sound and use it to track objects. It is essential for families and professionals to encourage the blind child to explore the immediate environment and then to develop systematic strategies for exploring the larger environment. Those who

Table 3. Development of the Ability to Search for and Recover Objects on the Basis of Sound Cues

Age at Which Behavior Develops	Behavior Demonstrated
23–28 weeks	If a sound-making object is removed from the infant, there is no vocalization or resistance.
27–36 weeks	Following contact with an object, the child makes random movements toward the object.
37–48 weeks	The search for a tactile object becomes organized; the child begins to understand that an object may be displaced in space independently of the child.
49 weeks	The child will reach for and recover an object on a sound cue alone and may creep toward the source of sounds.

In hand-over-hand modeling, the adult's hand physically guides the hand of the child.

Modeling can be used to help a child learn to scan systematically. Here braille readiness is developed as a young student learns to move his hands in a left-to-right sequence.

do not find an adaptive solution tend not to explore; they remain in the mouthing phase of development, during which the child uses the mouth as the primary mechanism for sensory exploration. It is important that blind children gain the experience of searching in the environment so that they may develop an understanding that objects exist permanently in space.

DEVELOPMENT OF TACTILE ABILITIES

Because blind children may tend to be passive without appropriate early intervention, it is important that the child learn to explore objects actively and thoroughly. A system for tactile exploration can be taught. Teaching systematic scanning of objects, in which one part at a time is explored completely and a starting reference point is designated, is one successful approach. This systematic scanning can be taught by a modeling method in which the adult's hands are placed over the child's to guide them.

It is especially important to be as thorough as possible in the exploration of items that are too big to hold in the hands. One method of approaching large items is to build concepts, adding one to another. For example, for the blind preschooler who is being helped to explore his or her parents' car, an explanation of the concept of door may precede exploration of the trunk, followed by familiarization with the hood. These concepts, combined with a ride in the car, help the blind child achieve a wholeness in conceptual understanding. It is important to help visually impaired children make connections between events and experiences in the environment.

When teaching concepts tactilely, it is best whenever possible to use real items rather than models. Too often, models bear little resemblance to the real item in terms of tactile experience (for example, although a piece of wax fruit may visually resemble the actual fruit, it will not be similar in touch or smell). The same is true for raised-line representations of pictures in books. One-dimensional representations are helpful for visual input but not as helpful for tactile representation. In most cases, the raised-line drawing is unrelated to the represented item in terms of tactile input.

BRAILLE AND TACTILE DISCRIMINATION

Braille is a system of reading that incorporates six dots into a braille cell; different configurations of dots represent different letters, parts of words, words, and marks of punctuation. Braille reading and writing require special paper, special equipment, special books, and specialized skills. Desirable prerequisites for braille reading include:

- Ability to interpret symbols
- Ability to locate top and bottom of a page
- Ability to move the hands in a left-to-right sequence
- Muscle control for light touch
- Ability to use both hands together
- Tactile discrimination.

Tactile discrimination skills can be taught. Instruction begins with simple, large objects and gradually progresses to smaller, more complex discrimination tasks that require sensitivity in the fingers. For example, six Ping-Pong balls placed in a six-cell egg carton may be used for the introduction of braille. Gradually smaller items will be used until the child can discriminate actual braille dots. The sequence of tactile discrimination development is:

- Awareness of tactile stimuli
- Tolerance of tactile stimuli
- Recognition of tactile stimuli (familiarity)
- Interpretation of tactile stimuli (awareness of purpose)
- Appropriate use of the stimuli.

Braille-reading readiness can be encouraged by using braille labels for toys, books, and personal storage areas to which young children have access even before they can read the braille code. Sighted children have much experience with the medium of print long before they are actually reading. Blind children need similar opportunities of exposure to braille. In addition, commercial and handmade books that have braille overlay and realistic tactile inserts for key words (that is, actual buttons are attached to the page, requiring the child to count buttons) can be introduced to encourage the association between symbols and words that hold meaning for the young visually impaired child. Several commercial braille readiness and reading programs are available that help to prepare the young blind child for future use of braille as a viable medium for reading. It may be beneficial to encourage the severely visually impaired child who has some degree of usable vision to experience both braille and print media. At the readiness level neither medium should be excluded; young children will profit from the exposure. Appropriate determinations concerning braille versus print should be made as the visually impaired child matures and tactile, visual, and cognitive abilities can be assessed.

ASSESSMENT CONSIDERATIONS

When assessing the developmental levels of blind and visually impaired children, tools similar to those used to assess sighted children may be used, but with adaptations. Assessment is difficult because most of the available tests have been standardized for sighted children, so they are not valid or reliable for the blind population. In addition, infant assessments are not generally good predictors of later function for the visually impaired child; therefore, results must be viewed with caution. For a list of developmental assessment instruments, see the resource section at the end of this book.

The assessment process is further complicated when visually impaired children with additional disabilities are involved. It is most difficult to interpret test results and to determine which disabilities are affecting which areas of development. Additional disabilities may also affect the visually impaired child's ability to respond to assessment procedures. It is important to examine aspects of the test and the child's performance that are dependent on visual cues, neurological function, and motor ability. The assessor should be able to distinguish between possible deficits due to neurological or motoric dysfunction and those that are attributable directly to the child's lack of vision.

INTERVENTION STRATEGIES FOR PROMOTING COGNITIVE AND CONCEPT DEVELOPMENT

Without appropriate intervention, some congenitally blind children will develop pervasive and severe developmental deviations that mimic infantile autism (Warren, 1984). A child's efficiency at substituting nonvisual modalities for vision will affect his or her development.

When working with a child in the home, the infant specialist does not necessarily need to enter the teaching situation with a set plan. It is more important for the specialist to be able to show the family that learning can take place within the home spontaneously and at natural times, when the child is most interested in an activity. When working with multiply impaired children, the home teacher must be cognizant that activities may need to be of short duration because of the shorter attention spans of young children with multiple disabilities. With several appropriate goals and objectives in mind, the specialist may develop an intervention plan in conjunction with the family in order to address pertinent family concerns and priorities. Intervention strategies are most easily implemented by families when they are incorporated into the existing daily routine. The following integrated strategies and suggestions may be useful in working on cognitive, concept, auditory, or tactile development with the visually impaired or multiply impaired child. The ages at which children are ready to develop the skills that are outlined have not been included here, in the belief that families should be more concerned with the individual abilities of their children than with the expectations associated with their children's age group. It should be noted in regard to these suggestions and others presented elsewhere in this book that children should not be left unattended with objects that could pose any danger to them. The use of mobiles, string, and objects that the child could place in his or her mouth should be carefully supervised.

Grasp/Hand Skills
- If reflexive grasp (automatic response) predominates, place the child on his or her stomach to push up on the hands, thus encouraging the child to open the palms.
- Place a variety of objects in the infant's hands.
- Securely hang objects in the crib with which the child will make contact accidentally; this will help the child gain the idea of locating objects and foster the expectation of objects' existence in the environment.
- Vary the child's experiences with textures, smells, and tastes to provide interest.
- Tie toys to the child's chair with a short string; gradually lengthen it.

When use of the thumb emerges, the following may be helpful:

- Gradually provide objects that are smaller and thinner than those used previously.
- Encourage self-feeding, the tearing of paper, and other activities that require the use of the hands.
- Put sticky tape on the child's fingers to encourage the use of the small muscles of the hand (have the child try to remove the tape).

Once pincer grasp (a grasp in which the thumb and forefinger work together) emerges, the following may be helpful:

- Use small edible objects to encourage the child's use of pincer grasp.
- Provide the child with toys that can be emptied or filled, such as blocks and a box.

Reaching
- To prompt the child to reach, work from behind; begin by moving the child's hand to the object and showing him or her how to pick up the object; gradually reduce the amount of guidance.
- Choose toys that make interesting sounds; be aware of the developmental sequence that children follow when reaching toward a sound made at ear level on one side (if there is no response, touch the object to the child's hand, turn his or her head toward it, and repeat the sound), made below ear level, above ear level, and made in front of the child.

Release of an Object from the Hand
- Use hand-over-hand motions for demonstration.
- Try sharing food to provide a motivation to release.
- Put sticky foods in the palm of the child's hand to exaggerate the motion of release.

Early Social Skills

- Provide the child with a wide variety of physical and verbal contact.
- Place the child in the center of an activity.
- Remember that although blind children need a great deal of stimulation, it is important not to overstimulate. Overstimulation may cause confusion and the child's eventual shutting out of sources of stimulation.

Concepts and Abstract Reasoning

- Provide the child with concrete experiences with shapes, textures, weights, and the like.
- Explain functions as well as names of objects.
- Describe rather than just name objects.

The following activities may help in developing categorization skills:

- Play simple matching games with the child.
- Work on the recognition of differences between two items.
- From a group of two similar objects and one dissimilar one, give the child one object and have him or her find which one of the two others it is like.
- From a group of two like and two different objects, give the child two different objects and have him or her match each with a like one.
- Have the child practice classifying objects by function and association.

The following activities may help develop problem-solving skills:

- Play guessing games with the child.
- Physically demonstrate to the child the use of one object to obtain another, such as pulling a string to get a toy.
- Provide the child with nesting and stacking toys.
- Allow the child to make decisions and to see the effects of those decisions.
- Provide explanations of what is happening in the child's environment.

The strategies suggested require the young visually impaired child to become increasingly involved in the immediate and expanding environments. With active involvement the child will experience many opportunities for the development of relevant concepts. Cognitive growth will enable the child to experience meaningful interactions in more aspects of life.

LANGUAGE DEVELOPMENT

Normal Language Development

Theories. From the beginning, children are interested in interacting with and learning about their environment. To promote language as well as cognitive development, it is important to provide input and stimulation that are responsive to their interests about the familiar as well as the novel and that are a little beyond their current level of ability.

Previously it was theorized that language acquisition occurred as children received reinforcement for attempting to talk and later were corrected by their parents. Speech therapists often use these techniques. However, children do not learn language in this way. If someone corrects a child's language, the child will not be able to use the feedback if he or she does not understand the principle behind the correction (Moskowitz, 1976; Tager-Flushberg, 1985).

Parents do not correct their young children's syntax, but they listen for what is true or not and reinforce the child's attempts to talk. Despite variability in the way adults talk to children who are acquiring language, most children acquire the major language milestones at comparable rates. Language acquisition—the active construction of language by children—occurs through interaction with the environment. The key is providing children with the opportunity to interact.

Preverbal Interactions. During the first year of life, the interactions in which sighted children engage lay the groundwork for language acquisition. Their eye contact with their parents reinforces the adults' efforts to interact with a preverbal partner. Initially, sighted children smile at any human face; then they learn to discriminate and smile selectively at their parents. Smiling reinforces parents' interactions with the child and helps parents and child to bond. At this stage, sighted children also learn how to attract attention and how to initiate and end interactions. The parent will notice and look for objects that seem to interest the child and will talk about them. By 10 or 11 months, children will point, use gestures, or establish eye contact to communicate what is of interest to them. Frequently, a parent may misunderstand the child's initial attempts to express him- or herself, but the child quickly develops strategies to repair these misunderstandings. For instance, the child may try to direct the parent's attention by looking at or leaning toward the object of interest.

Babbling and First Words. During the first 6 months, children begin to make sounds. This babbling lasts approximately 6 to 8 months. Between approximately 10 and 18 months of age, children acquire their first words. The words may not be identical to adult words (*bottle* may be *ba-ba*), but they are used in a consistent way, and it is important for parents to reinforce these early attempts to communicate. Parents often rely on visual information (for example, the child's gestures) to make sense of these early words.

Impediments to Language Development

The visual cues given by their children provide most parents with reinforcement to continue interacting with the children. Parents of blind children may need assistance in finding cues to which they can respond.

As already indicated, sighted children first smile at any human face, then discriminate and smile selectively at familiar faces. This behavior is reinforcing to parents. However, blind children do not smile as frequently or selectively as sighted children do. Parents of blind children may misinterpret this behavior and believe that their children have not adequately bonded to them, which may lead to reduced attempts on the part of parents to interact with their blind children.

In a number of ways, it is more difficult for parents to interact with a visually impaired child than with a sighted one. The parents of a visually impaired child cannot rely on visual cues such as eye gaze and gestures to communicate to them their child's interests. In addition, the blind child does not have the same strategies for attracting attention or correcting misunderstandings that a sighted child has. Blind children may tend to be fussy and given to tantrums as a result of not being understood.

Most linguists indicate that blindness need not result in major or long-term articulation problems. Apparently, the inability to see others' mouths is not a critical factor in language acquisition. The key is not how a child makes a sound but how others respond to it. A parent may have difficulty understanding what a blind child's babbling means. A blind child has a limited use of eye gaze and a limited repertoire of gestures which might help parents interpret their child's babbling.

Often, once blind children are verbal they demonstrate any of three characteristics in their speech. They may ask many questions, demonstrate echolalia, and make "off-the-wall" comments.

Questions. Blind children tend to ask many questions, sometimes inappropriately. It is important to be aware of the underlying function of the questions so that the child can find an alternate way to meet his or her needs. Some functions of these questions are gathering information, attracting attention, and responding to confusion or fear. It is important that children learn socially appropriate ways of achieving these ends. For example, even though questioning may be one effective means of gathering information, independent or assisted exploration of an object or concept should be encouraged in conjunction with questioning. A question can be an initially effective attention getter, but follow-up techniques must be developed (that is, moving closer to a person, conversing socially, and listening actively). Questions are often posed by the visually impaired child to receive reassurance of someone's physical presence. Adults should be sensitive to this need and attempt to provide verbal and emotional reassurances. Visually impaired children should be encouraged to express their feelings of confusion or fear directly rather than developing an overreliance on questioning.

Echolalia. Echolalia, the repetition of statements used by other people, is not a completely negative phenomenon. As with questions, it is important to determine the child's uses of echolalia and to respond to them. Echolalia can be a part of normal language development, or a rehearsal used to help process input. It may also be used as an attempt to initiate interaction. When a child does not appear to understand his or her echolalic speech, when it is not used for interactive purposes, and when the child does not begin to break down the echolalic speech and use it creatively, then it may be helpful to get some professional advice in order to reduce or extinguish the pattern effectively.

"Off-the-Wall" Comments. Many blind children have difficulty listening to and following conversations because of missed visual and social cues. They may make comments unrelated to the event at hand. Although it is common for all children to stray from conversations at times, if a visually impaired child seems to focus solely on his or her own interests rather than on conversations at hand, it may be helpful to let the child know when comments or behaviors are inappropriate and to offer appropriate alternatives for participating in social situations.

It is important to strive to help the young visually impaired child to develop communicative competence. For multiply impaired children who are not demonstrating expressive language, initial alternative communication techniques should be discussed with a language specialist. The use of communication boards, with which children can communicate their needs by pointing to specific pictures, by moving assorted objects on "calendar" boards, or by activating artificial speech phrases, may foster the development of expressive language. The introduction of a few basic sign-language words for communication purposes is another first step for children with deficits in expressive language. The ability to use language in a socially appropriate way has long-term implications for the visually impaired child in the areas of socialization, academics, self-esteem, and independence. Having high expectations for the young visually impaired child can be the first step toward the child's attainment of communicative competence. Both parents and professionals must expect and encourage young visually impaired children to communicate their needs, likes, and dislikes rather than anticipate and provide for a child's needs before the child has had an opportunity to express them.

Promoting Language Development: Intervention Strategies

The following strategies will help to promote language development in visually impaired children:

- *Teach parents alternate routes for interaction.* Additional physical contact, for instance, may help reinforce the child's smiling and babbling.
- *Listen and watch.* Assist the family in identifying and observing nonvisual cues about the child's interests and how to respond to these.
- *Maintain high expectations for the child's language.* Do not always guess the child's needs or wants but instead encourage the child to make his or her needs known.
- *Acknowledge the child's efforts to communicate.* A child's early attempts to communicate need to be encouraged. When parents and professionals imitate and expand on children's language, children are encouraged to continue talking.
- *Provide opportunities for exploration and listening.* Visually impaired children learn by listening and by exploring the environment. However, too much input can be overwhelming and can cause a child to tune out sounds in their surroundings.
- *Try to provide extra information about things that are discussed.* Instead of merely labeling, describe the persons and objects that are of interest to the child.
- *Provide hands-on experiences.* The language spoken to a visually impaired child needs to be reinforced with firsthand experiences. When visually impaired children understand language, they are less likely to be echolalic.
- *Respond to the ideas and feelings in the child's speech.* By paying careful attention to the visually impaired child's actions and the events taking place around him or her, others will be able to respond to the child's underlying intentions.
- *Express your feelings and put the child's feelings into words.* Visually impaired children cannot read feelings from the frowns, smiles, and expressions of others. Other persons' feelings need to be explained, and the child needs to be taught how to express his or her own feelings appropriately.

- *Try to expand on the child's existing language.* The child's attempts to communicate can be used as the basis for further communication. For instance, if a child says "ba-ba," the parent may respond with, "Yes, that is your bottle," and go on to describe it.
- *Assist the child in developing socially appropriate responses.* Attention should be paid to social skills. For instance, the child may be taught to listen to what other children are doing and to imitate their behavior when he or she wants to join in friends' play.
- *Do not attempt too much.* Try to teach one goal at a time, when the child is most receptive and interested.
- *Be supportive and encouraging.* It is important that interactions are fun for visually impaired children and that children talk about shared interests and enjoy interacting with one another. Respect the child's attempts to communicate.

Promoting Successful Peer Interactions

The following strategies promote positive peer interactions:

- *Provide informal, responsive training to nondisabled peers.* By responding to children's immediate concerns and questions about visual impairment, specialists can address issues that are most meaningful to the children. The process should be ongoing in order to maximize the children's learning potential.
- *Discuss visual impairments with the visually impaired child and with peers.* It is important to provide the visually impaired child with the means to explain his or her impairment to others and to take responsibility for his or her special needs. Peers need to understand the similarities and differences between themselves and their visually impaired peer. Help the child's peers to understand and accommodate appropriately without focusing solely on the disability.
- *Encourage the visually impaired child to display preferences.* Visually impaired children do not always provide the same reinforcing messages to peers as do sighted children. Specialists may need to prompt visually impaired children to verbalize their preferences, share toys, save a place for a friend, and put their feelings about other children into words.
- *Carefully monitor social interactions.* Examine both the rate and quality of interactions over time. It is desirable for peer interactions to increase in frequency and for roles played by both visually impaired and sighted children to be appropriate. To obtain an accurate picture of the visually impaired child's social experiences, careful, unobtrusive observation of interactions is required.

Visual impairment can have a profound impact on the development of cognition, concepts, and language. These developmental areas are essential building blocks in the formation of more complex skills and levels of learning. With appropriate individualized intervention, young visually impaired children may develop competencies that will enable them to parallel more closely the growth and development of their sighted peers.

Chapter 4

SOCIAL FOCUS: DEVELOPING SOCIOEMOTIONAL, PLAY, AND SELF-HELP SKILLS IN YOUNG BLIND AND VISUALLY IMPAIRED CHILDREN

CONTRIBUTORS

Diane L. Fazzi
Play and the Visually Impaired Child

Shirley A. Kirk
Self-Help Skills

Ruth S. Pearce
Early Childhood Development

Rona L. Pogrund
Functional-Skills Approach
Socioemotional Development

Sheila Wolfe
Play Skills Development

Learning to function as independently as possible in the world is a long-term goal for all visually impaired children. Developing a positive self-image as part of continuing emotional and social growth is a significant key to independent functioning. The impact of lack of vision on the development of socioemotional, play, and self-help skills is substantial. Most skills in these critical areas are learned incidentally by young sighted children as they observe those around them modeling appropriate social behaviors, interactions with others, and activities of daily living. In contrast, children with visual impairments do not automatically integrate skills in these important areas. The visually impaired child therefore needs specialized instruction in the areas of socialization, play, and self-help.

This chapter examines these unique areas of need by outlining typical landmarks in early childhood development and discussing the impact of vision loss on the visually impaired child's motility, autonomy, cognition, values, and ability to make emotional attachments. The three spheres of mastery necessary for all children to develop are mastery with others, mastery of objects, and mastery of the inner world of the self. These spheres, along with early social development and the development of independence and self-esteem in the visually impaired child, will be examined. The chapter addresses the importance of play in the life of all young children and focuses on the unique considerations in this area for the child with a visual impairment. The functional-skills approach to education will be analyzed, and applications to the young visually impaired population will be considered. Activities of daily living, which are some of the most functional skills of all leading to independence, are also discussed in this chapter.

EARLY CHILDHOOD DEVELOPMENT

Normal development of all children must include certain developmental landmarks, which can be affected by the presence of a disability. Major tasks to be accomplished lie in the areas of attachment, motility, autonomy, cognition, and values.

Attachment

Attachment in infancy is the mutual closeness between infant and caregiver that is achieved predictably by the infant and provides him or her with a sense of control. Attachment, and the control inherent in it, begins with the infant's first communications, including crying, smiling, vocalizing, clinging, reaching, and following.

Attachments begin positively, with the child's expectations of being able to draw the mother close. In time, however, attachment builds an increased sense of vulnerability when the mother leaves the child or the child leaves the mother. For instance, when the child learns to walk, at first he or she feels great excitement about the new ability, but soon elation is tempered by a fear of moving too far away from the mother—the toddler usually takes a few steps and then checks to see that the mother is still there. Vision plays an important role in the development of attachment. The sighted child continually uses visual cues to draw the caregiver closer and to stay connected during brief physical separations. Young sighted children also use the visual interpretation of facial expressions to determine whether the caregiver approves or disapproves of their actions.

Autonomy and Motility

Autonomy is knowledge of the self and the world and the ability to manipulate the world. This knowledge involves understanding that one is a separate entity from objects and others in the environment. Vision aids in the development of this understanding because it allows the simultaneous perception of items in the environment. Autonomy is supported by motility.

Differentiating the self from the world is difficult for blind children, and the ability to do so develops later for them. Blind children make all the postural achievements, such as sitting and standing, at the same time as their peers, but they do not move forward into the environment at the same time. Auditory signals alone are not enough to motivate movement. Through attachment, however, and increasing familiarity with and mastery of objects, it is possible to give the child the understanding that objects have permanence in space. Once children understand that an object exists even when it cannot be perceived in any way, they are able to image, or map, the environment in their minds.

Cognition

Cognition involves knowledge about the world. The child gains this knowledge by acting on the world and experimenting with it. Vision helps children organize information by enabling them to perceive an entire object or action at once. The blind child must use sense memories other than those provided through vision to organize information. These other senses are serial in nature (for example, although a person can hear many things simultaneously, he or she can interpret only one at a time) and so may not provide the whole understanding of the world afforded by vision.

Values

The development of values begins with a simple sense of good and bad. As early as 6 months of age, babies may resist having their diaper changed, and their mothers may respond irritably and forcefully. *Bad* and *angry* become equated without these words ever being used. Through these inevitable experiences the child develops the capacity to evaluate feelings and through this process learns how to interact with others.

The sighted child recognizes other people's feelings using a variety of cues, including facial expressions. The blind child recognizes auditory and tactile cues such as tone and level of sound and roughness of handling, but these cues do not have the organizing power of vision. With the help of teachers, parents must aid the blind child in putting together an evaluation system that enables the child to feel not only that he or she knows how to be good, but that even when he or she is bad, the child and parents will put the behavior in perspective and know that they and their relationship will survive the behavior.

THREE SPHERES OF MASTERY

The major life tasks are accomplished within three spheres, or areas: mastery with others, mastery of objects, and mastery of the inner world of the self. Mastery with others begins with the first contact with another person. Within this sphere the child learns that others may be able to validate his or her feelings. The communication of one's own needs and the understanding and prediction of the behavior of others are learned. The child also learns to ask for help and to seek approval and finds that negative feelings can be expressed safely. All these accomplishments imply attachment to another person.

Within the sphere of mastery of objects, the child learns to explore and to enjoy novelty. He or she learns to expect success, to tolerate defeat, to reason, and to use active investigation to establish self-esteem. The child begins to take pleasure in completing a task. Without autonomy, he or she cannot achieve the mastery of objects.

Within the sphere of the mastery of the inner world of the self, the child takes pleasure in his or her own body and knows what the body can do; he or she also takes pleasure in fantasy. The child becomes able to delay gratification, to deal with frustration and anxiety, and to avoid behaviors that are safety risks, such as leaning over a banister. Through fantasy, the child explores life and begins to learn how to deal with it.

All children must master certain developmental accomplishments, including attachment, autonomy, motility, cognition, and establishment of values. Mastery of these accomplishments leads to a healthier self-concept, which is the bridge to success in all of life's challenges.

SOCIOEMOTIONAL DEVELOPMENT

Early Social Development

Most parent-child interactions are predicated on the exchange of eye contact. If there is no such eye contact, interaction is difficult to maintain. The parents of blind children often view their babies as unresponsive, and so may withdraw. The parent of a blind child must look, or be taught to look, for other signs of recognition, such as tension in the baby's hands or changes in sucking.

The development of smile behavior follows a definite course. Although sighted infants begin smiling near the end of the first month, a social smile—a smile in response to another person—does not appear until children are 2 to 3 months old. This smile is often elicited by the caregiver's or another person's voice and is typically indiscriminate. A true smile, one that is selectively used to express joy in recognition of the mother or primary caregiver, begins to stabilize between the fifth and sixth months of life. After 6 months there is a noticeable decrease in smiling directed toward unfamiliar people (Warren, 1984).

In early development, blind children's smiling behaviors are similar to those of sighted children. At this stage smiles are effectively elicited by tactile and auditory stimuli. At 2 to 3 months, when smiles seem to be visually elicited for sighted children, smiling behavior appears to remain more reflexive in nature for the blind baby. However, in blind children, smiling during the second quarter of the first year is more selective to the voices of the child's parents than it is in sighted children (Fraiberg, 1970).

As smiling behaviors are visually reinforced by returned smiles, the sighted infant begins to imitate facial expressions and to acquire a variety of nonverbal ways to convey feelings. Blind infants do not receive reciprocal smiling reinforcement at this readiness stage, which may diminish the amount of smiling exhibited unless the child receives adequate haptic (touch-related) stimulation as substitute reinforcement (Fraiberg, 1977). Most of the world of nonverbal communication is not readily accessible to the blind child.

Since blind children do not smile as frequently or intensively as sighted children, their social interactions may be affected. In general, blind infants do not initiate affectionate games or indicate with gestures the desire to be held. These behaviors may be due to the blind child's inability to see him- or herself as the cause of an action. It is important to realize that the absence of a response in the blind child does not imply the absence of potential, and the degree and intensity of smiling are not necessarily accurate indicators of the extent of attachment. Neither is lack of response always indicative of the child's abilities. The blind child may have a tendency to listen and lie very still without making outward responses of reaching out and touching meaningfully. The lack of facial and gestural cues, however, may be misread by the parents as disinterest, unfriendliness, or apathy. These behaviors may interfere with the formation of the relationship between the parents and the infant. There is a risk that the parents may unconsciously minimize interactions with their child because of the infant's apparent unresponsiveness. Ironically, the visually impaired infant needs more contact and stimulation than does the sighted one. These early bonds of human attachment form the basis of feelings of being loved and valued and are a necessity for a positive self-image.

Separation Anxiety

Sighted children see their parents leaving the room and reappearing and begin to develop separation anxiety—anxious feelings caused by being separated from a caregiver—and thus exhibit attachment bonds. This whole process of exhibiting separation anxiety and forming attachments may be delayed for blind children. Among children who are blind, the development of a communication system is delayed until an auditory or tactile system can be established. It is extremely important for parents to give the blind infant auditory and tactile cues when they are leaving or returning so that the signals are paired by the child with the security of being able to distinguish the parents from other people. At approximately 7 months of age the infant who is blind from birth is able to distinguish his or her mother's skin from that of strangers by touch and reacts with anxiety to the difference. When being held, the blind child is also able to react to postural differences between his or her mother and a stranger.

Independence and Self-Esteem

There are substantial differences in the development of independence in sighted and blind children. Overprotection of the visually impaired child restricts the child's exposure to the environment and limits his or her opportunities to explore and manipulate it. Overprotection interferes with the child's development of initiative, independence, and recognition of his or her abilities. Responsibility and independence lead to further successful experiences and a broadening of self-competence, self-satisfaction, self-esteem, and pride. For example, allowing the young visually impaired child to make decisions about clothing and food, to have responsibility for picking up and putting away toys, and to participate in family chores helps develop a sense of competence. If opportunities for experiencing competence and success are limited, the child does not develop an accurate picture of his or her abilities and goes out into the world with hesitancy and reticence. It is through exploration and action that a child discovers more completely his or her individual skills and strengths, all of which contributes to a healthy self-concept. Self-esteem and perceived competence are the keys to meeting life's demands successfully. Competence, which gives the child a feeling of control, mediates failure.

Learned helplessness is the feeling of lack of control over the events in one's life. If family members and teachers do everything for the blind child and make all the decisions for the child, learned helplessness results, creating passivity in the visually impaired child. Shyness is the result of inaction, as the child always waits for others to initiate contact in social situations. Passivity causes inaction, and inaction contributes to the social isolation and lack of positive social interactions that are so common among visually impaired children.

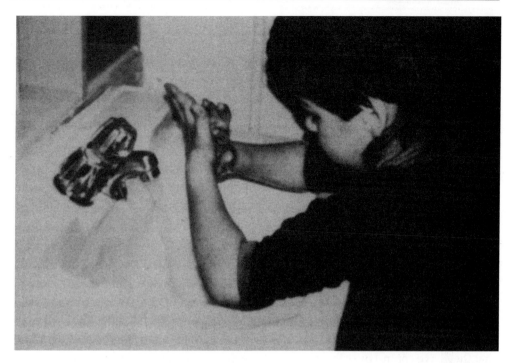

Taking responsibility for personal hygiene is a positive step toward independence and self-esteem for a child.

The self-esteem "circle" is as follows: A person's self-esteem affects performance; performance, in turn, shapes self-perception and the perceptions of others; other people's opinions have a direct impact on self-esteem; and self-esteem affects the individual's ability to perform. The early years in the life of a visually impaired child play the most significant role in determining this pattern, which may hold long-term implications for the child.

All children struggle with such basic questions as "Who am I?" "Am I lovable?" "Where do I belong?" and "Can I handle it?" The visually impaired child who experiences devaluing or negative reactions from others in the social environment may find it more difficult to get satisfactory answers to these fundamental questions. When any child is made to feel strange, different, unwanted, incapable, or inadequate, self-esteem will be diminished.

Social Skills Development

Social skills, learned incidentally by most sighted children, must be systematically taught to the visually impaired child. For a young child, feeling competent in social situations evolves from having a positive self-image and from having the tools to interact appropriately. For example, teaching young visually impaired children to hold their heads up and "look" at others when spoken to, to invite others to join them in play, and to keep their hands to themselves when they first meet someone helps make them more socially accepted by peers. A structured intervention plan may be helpful in ensuring age-appropriate social development for the visually impaired child. Assisting the child with specific strategies for use in social interactions, facilitating appropriate behaviors, helping eliminate inappropriate mannerisms, supporting good hygiene and age-appropriate dress, and helping the child to feel competent and self-sufficient are all strategies that promote positive social development.

The visually impaired child may show an absence of aggression, may be passive, or may resort to tantrums or helpless behavior in stressful situations. These behaviors may occur because the blind child is unable to express aggression and instead regresses because he or she is unable to observe how others express similar feelings. It is important to teach visually impaired children ways to discharge their anger appropriately so they can feel that they have control in a variety of situations. It is the feeling of control that facilitates the development of the child's self-esteem more than anything else. Families and teachers who take control of each situation (for example, intervening every time a peer teases), and who do not give the visually impaired child choices and opportunities to take risks and even experience failure at times, are depriving the child of a highly significant aspect of socioemotional development. For visually impaired children to develop socially, they need to feel good about themselves, to understand the differences their visual impairment creates, to learn social skills that will make them more accepted by others, to know their own abilities and limitations, and to feel that they have control over themselves and their environment.

DEVELOPMENT OF PLAY SKILLS

Play has clearly been identified by experts in the field of child development as a primary avenue for children to learn about themselves and the world around them. Through play, children act out and lay the foundation for their immediate as well as future behaviors and beliefs. Because of the key role of play in child development, it should be a primary focus of early intervention. It is also important to think about and respond to the child's need for play—just for the sake of play.

To be "playing" might mean taking part in, doing; causing, acting on, acting out; pretending, imitating, creating; or toying with life's options and alternatives. Because play takes many different forms, it is helpful to think of it along a continuum that includes its many characteristics. Some of the spectrums of play that might be considered include:

- Social to asocial
- Passive to active
- Cooperative to competitive
- Spontaneous to imitative
- Quiet to loud
- Organized to disorganized
- Repetitive to very quickly changing.

Both ends of each play spectrum must be considered and valued as a part of the whole. Some children may be very good social players but may be unable to entertain themselves and experience asocial, or solitary, play. In this situation, it would be helpful to guide the child toward learning more independent play. It is of course important to respect individual personality differences and play preferences.

Stages, Phases, and Changes in Play

One way of categorizing different kinds of play includes dividing the concept into four major stages:

- sensorimotor
- manipulative
- symbolic
- game playing.

The ages at which these stages occur vary widely according to the individual child's development.

Sensorimotor Play. Sensorimotor play is often called physical play. It is marked by attention to movement, sensation, exploration, and awareness of how all sensations relate to each other. There is much emphasis on this period as a time when the young child gains understandings in a very physical way.

Manipulative Play. The emphasis of manipulative play is on the complex aspects and details of play. Actions are taken in regard to objects in order to gain control and understanding of them. At this stage the child pays a great deal of attention to detail and intricacies.

Symbolic Play. Symbolic play involves fantasy and creative play, which are usually learned from watching someone else. Symbolic play involves the use of symbols to represent objects that are not available or present in the play situation. This stage is extremely important in helping the child progress through attachment, separation, and individuation.

Game Playing. This stage, which involves pacing, following rules, scoring, and other methods of organization, is usually thought of as occurring when the child is older. Actually, however, this style of play can also be observed in very young children (for instance, the child who plays peek-a-boo adheres to a set of rules and paces his or her responses).

Each of these stages or aspects of play mesh with one another through development and the child's ability to draw on a wide repertoire of play behaviors. Rather than being concerned about the age at which each type of play emerges, it is important to consider the variety of toys, the duration of play sessions, and the variety of types of play when determining a child's competence in play (Bailey & Woolery, 1989).

Assessment of Play Skills

Although many commercially available developmental assessments exist, the skills designated as checkpoints in development do not reflect the qualitative aspects of a child's overall development. Therefore, careful, ongoing observations of a child's play and playfulness are necessary. The following are guidelines for assessing a child's play:

- Gather information from parents, other family members, and caretakers about the child's play; ask open-ended questions like, "How does your child play?" or, "How would you describe _____'s play?"
- Observe other people playing with the child. Watch for interaction, timing, pacing, and emotions.
- Observe the child in both structured and unstructured play situations.
- Observe the child's spontaneous play.
- Observe the child's responses to familiar as opposed to new play activities.
- Observe the child at a variety of times during the day or week to account for and consider his or her different emotional and alertness states.
- Observe the pattern, organization, or theme of the child's play.
- Observe the quality and timing of the child's play in response to parent-child and child-parent interactions.
- Observe the child's learning preference, style, and problem-solving strategies.

Impact of Vision Loss

In young visually impaired children the absence of visual stimuli correlates with a lower level of motivation to move through the environment, manipulate toys, and initiate play with peers. Vision loss makes it more difficult for children to understand and organize objects and events in the environment. Thoughtfully chosen toys, materials, and activities can have a positive impact on the development of play.

Families may need to retrain themselves to include nonvisual forms of play when spending time with their visually impaired child, since typical visual cues and environmental stimuli may be partially or completely lacking. Providing sound cues for games such as tickling the child can help him or her anticipate actions and reactions. Using inflection, pitch, and vocal pacing may provide motivation for young children to participate actively in reciprocal play.

The young child's motivation to explore the environment is inhibited by the lack of vision; similarly limited are the child's abilities to engage people and to learn through imitation. Visually impaired children also need structured opportunities for movement and outdoor play, which will form a foundation for independent mobility.

The presence of additional impairments may compound the difficulties associated with play. Physical disabilities may exacerbate the child's lack of desire or ability to move, act on, master, and control the physical environment. Neurological-perceptual impairments may further hamper the child's ability to gather, organize, interpret, and respond to environmental input. Cognitive delays may limit the visually impaired child's understanding of the interactions, events, and relatedness of life experiences. Additional health problems may limit the stamina needed to explore, play, and learn.

In accordance with safety precautions, educational toys need to be selected and play opportunities provided after thorough consideration in order to maximize the potential benefits of play for visually impaired children. The following principles should be kept in mind:

- Materials should be stimulating for young visually impaired children.

- Materials should be easily manipulated, age appropriate, and developmentally challenging.
- Materials should provide opportunities for functional play.
- Patterned objects, especially black-and-white concentric circles, are interesting for the infant with low vision to look at.
- Mobiles should contain visually, tactilely, and aurally stimulating items and should be placed at nose level, within the child's reach but tied securely.
- The environment should be organized so that toys and stimulating objects are close to the visually impaired child.
- Smaller toys should be placed in a shallow container or on a tray so that they are not easily lost.
- Secured suction toys are helpful for children with motor control problems.
- Soft, cuddly fur toys may be tactilely unpleasant for some young visually impaired children.
- Ordinary household items (that is, spoons, containers, hairbrushes, sponges, and so on) can be motivating, manipulative toys that possess functional qualities.

Early positive interactions with peers are important for the development of a child's social and play skills.

Young visually impaired children have opportunities for play in the home and at day care and in preschool programs. If family members, extended family, friends, and professionals are sensitive in providing play opportunities that foster reciprocity and active participation on the part of the visually impaired child, they may help create a foundation for future social interactions.

An organized intervention strategy is often an essential component of a successful preschool program for visually impaired children. Visually impaired preschoolers—especially those children with severe vision loss who lack the ability to use visual and imitation cues—do not necessarily adopt interactive play styles. It is often difficult for blind and visually impaired children to interact appropriately with their peers. In play situations involving sighted peers, the visually impaired child is often unable to keep track of the activities in which the sighted children are involved. These difficulties are compounded when gross motor activities are involved. Attempts made by sighted children to engage the visually impaired child are often met with behaviors that may be interpreted as demonstrating a lack of interest, responsiveness, and enthusiasm (for example, dropped head, rocking, echolalic response, and the like). Sighted children may quickly lose interest in playing with a child who is perceived as unusual or different.

When visually impaired children play with one another, their interactions often appear to lack synchronization. In fact, two visually impaired children who appear to be playing together may actually be engaged in a form of parallel play. As children miss cues from each other, they may lose interest in maintaining peer interactions, which often results in an increased egocentricity in the play of the visually impaired child.

The types of play visually impaired children engage in are typically different from those of their sighted peers. Young visually impaired children exhibit a tendency toward greater frequency of manipulative and fantasy play, while exhibiting fewer instances of functional and dramatic play (Parsons, 1986). An example of functional play is using a "child-size" model kitchen set to simulate cooking and cleaning activities. Dramatic play is exemplified by acting out a familiar role, such as playing "doctor and nurse."

Early-interventionists may help to expand the play repertoire of young visually impaired children in several ways. Orientation and mobility (O&M) specialists should familiarize the child with the play setting, indoors and out, including some of the toys and playground equipment in the setting. If the visually impaired child is able to manipulate competently much of the available play equipment, it may help to increase his or her acceptance by peers. The young child need not have mastery of all the toys and equipment; it is more important that he or she begin to develop a systematic approach to the exploration of new objects of interest.

Mediating the visually impaired child's play experiences with other children may initially be helpful to the child. For example, the teacher can encourage sighted preschoolers to describe their activities verbally as an alternative to pointing or other nonverbal gestures. The interventionist can encourage visually impaired preschoolers to express their inability to understand visually what is happening by saying, "I can't see that—tell me what you're doing," or can encourage participation in activities in which both sighted and visually impaired children are interested and feel competent (for example, movement-to-music activities in a well-defined area; games requiring sighted children to wear blindfolds, such as pin-the-tail-on-the-donkey; and climbing activities with sighted children for visually impaired children who have good motor coordination). Without being directive, adults can help bridge the gaps in social interaction often inherent in young visually impaired children's play. The specialist must be careful to avoid becoming the central focus of the child's play, because engaging in verbal interactions with adults may become preferred to socializing with peers.

Families can help their visually impaired child by involving him or her in household activities, thus fostering a better understanding of the functional uses of common household items. For example, a child who has been involved in making pudding with the family, from start to finish, may be more likely to engage in functional play involving "pretend" stirring, pouring, and eating. With lots of hands-on experience, young children can develop competencies that can extend into more complex forms of play.

Play is an important component of learning for all children. Visually impaired children can extend their choices of play and enjoy satisfying social interactions with their peers if they are supported at home and in school to experience a variety of activities and to initiate appropriate peer relationships in their lives.

DEVELOPMENT OF SELF-HELP SKILLS

The area of self-help is one in which young children begin to take care of their basic needs and gain feelings of independence. The term *skills* in relation to self-help refers to activities that are distinct and segmented within each area of the daily routine. *Activities of daily living* is a much more descriptive term and its usage in regard to the abilities encompassed by *self-help* is preferred. There are no developmental skills that are required specifically for the activities of daily living; such activities rely on other developmental areas.

Center-Based vs. Home-Based Training

In regard to early intervention, activities of daily living for young visually impaired children are addressed both at home and within center-based programs. Cooperation between the school and the home is crucial for achieving consistent, successful programming. There are basic differences in the way instruction is approached in each of these settings.

The center-based environment offers a great deal of versatility and may allow for the building of an entire curriculum around activities of daily living. These activities can be easily generalized to a variety of instructional times during the day. It is necessary to create relevance for the activities addressed, however. For instance, the daily activities of eating, washing, and using vision can be addressed as the occasions for them arise naturally during snack time and lunch. Most training in center-based programs is goal oriented, leading to higher levels of independence in regard to self-help.

Training within the home needs to be less directive than that provided in a center-based program. The instructor may use modeling and suggestion. The majority of work in the home is with the parents, who then incorporate practice within the daily routine of the child and family. It is important for the teacher to learn to ask questions to elicit information and to establish rapport. Cultural differences must be taken into account, and information the teacher provides should be able to be incorporated easily into the family's life-style.

Primary Activities

Bathing, dressing, eating, and becoming toilet trained are primary activities of daily living for the child. There are many methods of extending these activities to a variety of settings so that the child will have a chance to practice and generalize the skills involved in these activities. These methods vary with the age of the child, and the age at which a child is ready to learn these skills varies greatly.

Bathing. Some babies do not like bath time. It is helpful to keep the baby partly covered and to bathe him or her with a cloth in a warm, supportive environment. Setting up a routine around bathing helps build anticipation for the child and creates order; these are building blocks for language development. For teachers working in the home, it is therefore important to help the family discover their own daily rituals.

Bath time can also be used to enhance the child's motor development and to help him or her learn about the body. Conversation can be extended to include discussions about body parts and their actions. Concepts such as wet and dry, in and out, or warm and cold can be pointed out and worked on naturally during bath time. Practicing O&M skills can be incorporated into such activities as locating the bathroom from various points in the house and exploring the sensory cues available.

Dressing. Dressing involves both removing and putting on clothes. For the infant, it is important to give cues prior to and during the removal of clothing. Body awareness can be developed by playing body-part-naming games. A Mylar mirror or Plexiglas near the changing area may be useful to help create an interest in surroundings for the visually impaired child with some vision.

As soon as the child can sit up alone, activities related to dressing should be carried out while the child is sitting to give him or her vestibular stimulation (movement of the fluid in the inner ear) and a new orientation to pulling clothes on or off. It is important to use words and directional terms that are literally accurate when talking with the child. For example, "your socks are on the bed" is more accurate than "your socks are over here."

At home it is often helpful for parents to choose the appropriate time for working with the child on dressing in light of time restraints. For instance, in a busy household with several young children, morning may not be the best time for a parent to work with the child. Timing is also important in a center-based program. It is important to choose natural, logical times during the day to work on skills related to dressing and undressing. For instance, arrival at school, bathroom time, or preparing to go outside are appropriate times for addressing this area and are also times when the relevance of the activity is clear. Broader extensions of getting dressed and undressed include experience with putting clothes away or hanging them up, understanding concepts of clean and dirty, and separating, washing, and folding clothes.

Choices are important, and the child's decision-making skills can be developed by presenting him or her with simple choices, such as which of two shirts will be worn. Decisions about clothing can be made on the basis of texture, design, sleeve length, style, and color. For the blind child, developing a system of marking clothes and for storing clothing is important, and strategies that can be formulated at a very young age can be used for a lifetime.

Feeding. When working with parents on feeding their child, it is important for the vision specialist to work with other professionals, such as a doctor, nurse, or occupational therapist. Keeping the visually impaired infant upright, with head tipped slightly forward and well supported (almost facing the mother), may facilitate easier breast-feeding. When the infant is between 4 and 6 months old, the positioning of the child is a primary consideration. Traditional, semireclined positioning may not be the most effective breast- or bottle-feeding position for visually or multiply impaired infants who have sucking, swallowing, or head-control problems. Placing the infant upright in a special seat or corner of a chair or couch may offer added support and free the caretaker's hands for bottle-feeding. Although the technique just mentioned may facilitate easier feeding for infants who have difficulties, holding and cuddling the infant before and after feeding are important for the bonding process and should not be overlooked.

It may be helpful to use fingers to support the baby's mouth if the infant has difficulty mouthing the nipple or spoon. Sucking can be encouraged by gently rubbing the baby's cheeks or by gently stimulating the inside of the infant's mouth with a finger.

To help the visually impaired child make connections between events, it is useful to give specific auditory and tactile cues about what is happening prior to and during feeding. Body awareness can be enhanced during feeding with a focus on stimulating the mouth and facial area.

Feeding problems begin with games of control, in which the parent and child fight over when, how, what, and how much the child should eat. A control struggle can be avoided by learning to "read" the child's cues (such as the signal for when he or she has had enough food) and responding simply and clearly to them. It is sometimes helpful, if there is concern about the amount the child is eating, to consider the amount consumed within the last 72 hours rather than focusing on one meal.

For an older child who is able to use a high chair, feeding activities can incorporate exploration, tactile experiences, and cause-and-effect experiments (tipping over a bowl or throwing utensils on the floor to see what happens, hands in the food, and the like). This time can be used for concept development in a variety of areas including those relating to texture (for example, of various foods, liquids, napkins, and trays), receptive language (descriptions of events and foods), and body awareness. For the preschool-aged child, it is easy to develop extended activities around feeding, including cooking (which incorporates fine motor and social skills), going to the market, science (measuring, comparing items), and taste or sensory awareness activities.

Choice of foods is important. Commercially available "junior foods" often precipitate feeding problems because children become confused by their texture, which is neither solid nor liquid. It is better to grind regular table food for the child. This method helps the child make the transition to the table because the texture of food is more uniform and predictable, and the child will be accustomed to the flavors in the family's food.

As a general rule, if the child indicates he or she wants solid food, solid food should be given. Some children will eat slightly mashed table food rather than entirely solid food. Young children may have sophisticated tastes, which should be respected. For the visually impaired child, a wide variety of tastes, smells, and textures adds to the inducement to eat.

For the toddler and preschooler, the primary goals in feeding are independence and competence. Competence comes with instruction and practice. Independence comes with confidence and trust in the child's abilities to carry out the task. It is important to provide an environment for working on feeding that allows for "safe failure." If it seems that the world is ending because the child made a mess, the child will not try the task again.

Toilet Training. Early toilet training is not imperative. It is not unusual for sighted and visually impaired children not to be trained by 3 years of age. It is important to communicate this to parents and to encourage them to relax about toilet training.

When children are ready to be trained, they will indicate in some way (for instance, pulling at diapers) that they are uncomfortable with wet or soiled diapers. It is important to be alert to such signals.

It is sometimes helpful for parents to begin training by taking the child with them to the toilet. The child should also be checked to determine when he or she is wet and dry to estimate the time when a visit to the toilet will most likely next be needed. It is important for the parents to maintain a relaxed, positive, nonchalant attitude toward the training. If the child senses that the training provokes stress, a power struggle may ensue. Toileting and eating are two of the few things a child can control in his or her life. The greater the reaction that a child with little power receives from the parent regarding these two activities, the more stubborn and determined to gain control he or she may become. As the child reaches preschool age, additional toileting considerations need to be addressed. For example, blind boys may need practice in order to learn to urinate into the toilet. Utilizing the base of the toilet or edge of the urinal as guidelines for the placement of the feet may help the young boy line up to prevent accidents. Orientation to soap, toilet paper, paper towels, sinks, and trash cans in preschool or day care center bathrooms should be given if independent toileting is to occur.

Techniques for Teaching Activities of Daily Living

In teaching activities of daily living, the emphasis is too often on task completion, making it difficult to maintain an emphasis on the process involved in acquiring the abilities for the task. The following techniques are useful for teaching daily living activities:

- *Task analysis.* Task analysis is useful as a method of approaching problem solving and provides a strategic approach if the child has difficulties with an activity. Task analysis involves breaking down a task, such as tying shoelaces, into small sequential steps and teaching one step at a time.

- *Backward chaining.* In backward chaining, the instructor alone carries out procedure of a task except the last step, which the child completes; th prompted to complete more and more of the task, progressing backward entire task is mastered, while the adult's participation gradually lessens. I for tasks such as dressing.
- *Modeling.* Modeling a behavior, which encourages imitation of a technique on the part of the child, is most effective for very young children with some degree of vision. It is useful for teaching skills such as how to hold a spoon.
- *Motoring.* Motoring, a technique of physical prompting, such as using hand-over-hand teaching or physically helping a child progress through the full or partial motions of an activity, may help children who have very limited or no vision to learn specific techniques and movements involved in daily living tasks. Motoring is useful for teaching a child such techniques as holding a washcloth and locating the soap when bathing.
- *Demonstration.* Demonstration is similar to modeling except that it is used to teach a task rather than a behavior. Demonstrating an activity is not always effective, as young children may lose interest in an activity in which they do not participate. It is helpful if the instructor focuses his or her attention more on the activity than on the child during demonstration, as this directs the child's attention to the activity. Demonstration is useful for teaching the child with low vision such tasks as stirring ingredients for a recipe.
- *Reinforcement.* Positive reinforcement is helpful in any activity; it can be used most effectively with other methods. (Reinforcement is discussed further in Chapter 5.)

Children with multiple impairments may require additional assistance in learning and performing many activities of daily living. Patience should be exercised in order to give the child more time to attempt completion of an activity. More motoring and physical prompting may be needed to assist the child with additional disabilities. Ultimately, questions regarding the multiply impaired child's potential for independent functioning may have to be addressed. Partial participation in activities of daily living may promote self-esteem and dignity for some students, if it is balanced with full participation in other activities. It is important to avoid limiting expectations of ultimate self-sufficiency at an early age because many children eventually master some of the activities of daily living in spite of mental or physical disabilities.

Activities of daily living are used throughout life. As indicated earlier, the goals of instruction in activities of daily living are to establish both competence and independence.

A FUNCTIONAL CURRICULUM APPROACH

It is important to be aware of varying educational philosophies. As a team member, the O&M specialist, teacher of visually impaired students, or early childhood educator must understand the philosophy of other team members, both to communicate effectively with other members of the team and to present the case for using certain intervention techniques.

The traditional developmental and remedial models used in education may not always be appropriate for work with all children, especially those with multiple disabilities. The developmental model suggests that a milestone is a prerequisite for a higher-order milestone and that all children must follow the same predictable sequence of normal growth and development. According to the remedial model, there are certain skills that are "normal," and teachers should determine the deficits in skills and design instructional programs to remediate the deficits. All children do not follow the same patterns of growth and development. The functional-skills model is based on the belief that there are certain skills that are practical and critical for severely impaired individuals to learn regardless of their developmental or mental ages. It does not require children to learn "prerequisite" skills, teaches them only the functional skills they need, and allows them to participate in activities in natural environments. A more functional approach to education may better meet the needs of many children with severe disabilities. Aspects of this model may also be of benefit to visually impaired children.

Background

The functional-skills approach commonly used in the education of severely impaired children emerged as a philosophy in the 1970s (Brown, Nietupski, Hamre-Nietupski, 1976). The functional-skills model is based on the principle of normalization, or making available to all severely handicapped persons patterns of life and conditions of everyday living that are as close as possible to regular circumstances and ways of life (Nirje, 1969).

The functional curriculum focuses on implementing programs and developing skills in regard to five basic domains: domestic activities, recreational and leisure activities, vocational pursuits, activities in the community, and interaction with nondisabled persons. The functionality of a skill can be determined by asking the following question (Falvey, 1986): "If a student does not learn to perform a particular skill, will someone else have to do it for her or him?" This question should also be asked when prioritizing skills and objectives. If the answer is yes, the skill should be made a priority. On the basis of this approach, learning mobility skills to go to the bathroom independently becomes a higher priority than putting a puzzle together.

Application to Visually Impaired Children

There are a variety of ways in which the principles of a functional approach may be applied to the visually impaired and multiply impaired infant and preschool population.

Use of Chronologically Age-Appropriate Materials and Activities. Age-appropriate materials and activities can be determined by observing nondisabled children of the same age as the child with a disability. Just because a 4-year-old child tests at the 20-month level does not mean he or she will not enjoy other activities for 4 year olds. The activities in which a child engages contribute to others' perception of the child. The competency-deviancy hypothesis states that the more competent a person is perceived to be, the more deviance he or she is allowed (for instance, the "eccentric" behavior or dress of a rock star would be perceived as weird rather than glamorous if carried out or worn by a mentally impaired person [Gold, 1980]). When a child is given age-appropriate materials, an appearance of competence is being provided, and social interactions may increase for the child.

Use of Parent Inventory. It is critical to ask parents of visually impaired infants and preschoolers what they feel is important and what they want for their child. If the inventory of their concerns is constructed carefully, functional priorities can be identified. Educational objectives can be built around this information.

Future Environments. When working with an infant in the home, it is important to determine what activities will enhance the child's ability to function in the preschool classroom. If the child is in preschool, it is important to look at skills needed for kindergarten survival, such as taking turns, standing in line, and the like. The teacher should always be working toward functioning in future environments. The best way to find out what may be needed in the child's next environment is to observe it ahead of time to see what expectations the child's teacher may have for the children.

Use of Functional Activities. Some of the activities used in visual-efficiency training can be accomplished functionally. It is useful to analyze the environment and each skill on a developmental checklist and then to find ways to functionalize the skill to the task in which the child needs to use it, by teaching the visual skill in a relevant and meaningful context of daily living instead of simply as part of an isolated visual task. Promoters of the functional philosophy believe that there is no time to waste on nonfunctional activities. According to this perspective, instead of having the child do a nonfunctional scanning task as part of visual-efficiency training, it is preferable to have the child scan the toy shelf for the place to put a favorite toy.

Use of Natural Times to Teach Skills. Eating, dressing, and other daily living skills can be taught at natural times in natural contexts, rather than at nonrelevant times. For instance, undressing can be taught when the child is getting ready for toileting rather than at an artificially scheduled time.

Community-Referenced Instruction. Preschoolers can be taught environmental concepts and be provided a variety of experiences in the community. O&M training has its basis in community-referenced training. Such training is based on the premise that traveling to a grocery store or fast-food restaurant is more meaningful than simulating those places in the preschool classroom.

Vocational Training. It is important to begin thinking about the vocational domain early. Vocational education at the preschool level includes training in attending to a task, understanding concepts of time, following rules, and beginning simple jobs at home and in the classroom.

Interaction with Nondisabled Peers. Visually impaired children can be integrated with nondisabled peers at various times during the day. This interaction may occur with other children in the neighborhood, in a day care setting, in a regular preschool, or in a reverse integration program at a special preschool for visually impaired children. It is important, however, to provide social skills instruction in addition to opportunities for integration, as visually impaired children will not acquire these skills simply by associating with others. Visual modeling, which sighted children use to learn about appropriate social skills, may be limited or totally absent for the visually impaired child. Specialized social skills training is necessary for visually impaired children to be able to integrate successfully with children who do not have visual impairments.

Partial Participation. Partial participation and adaptations can be used on a variety of levels. For instance, using Velcro closures on shoes is an example of an adaptation that may allow a young child to participate partially in dressing him- or herself. Young visually impaired children can also participate in many sports and games partially, even if a vision loss prevents full participation. For example, a blind child can be the caller in the game "Red Rover."

Precautions in Using a Functional Approach

Issues about which the teacher should be aware when working with visually impaired infants and preschoolers within the functional model include:

- Visually impaired children often demonstrate early developmental delays, but they tend to progress through a normal developmental sequence. It is important to use caution when deciding to abandon a developmental curriculum totally. A critical question is, "When do we leave the expectation of normal development?"
- Because visually impaired children do not incidentally learn many of the things that sighted children do and do not easily benefit from the modeling of social skills, full-time attendance in a regular educational program is not always the best choice. There are many skills that must be taught by a qualified specialist who understands the impact of vision loss. Many visually impaired children need specialized skill development, often in a separate setting, during the early years if they are to succeed in integrated settings later. Learning critical specialized skills should not be sacrificed in favor of total integration in the preschool years.
- Because the functional-skills model is based on the needs of the moderately and severely impaired population, it does not adequately address academic skills needed by visually impaired children without cognitive limitations. It also does not address the specialized skills needed by many blind students to have access to the regular academic curriculum, such as a knowledge of braille, the Nemeth code, listening skills, and so on.
- Some of the techniques used in visual-efficiency training do not appear to be functional, yet they facilitate the use of vision for functional activities later. For example, stimulating the visual response system of a young visually impaired child with multiple impairments with the use of penlights and bright shiny objects may be a necessary first step to get the child to use vision. As the visual responses of fixating and tracking are developing, these skills can be simultaneously used to follow the spoon at feeding time, a more functional, though less visually motivating, activity. Many proponents of the functional-skills model do not understand this aspect of visual development and resist the use of visual training activities. Experts in the field of visual impairment may need to explain the rationale for using activities that stimulate visual development to others who do not understand the visual process.

For optimal visual development and efficient use of vision, visually impaired children need intensive visual training exercises in addition to training to improve their more functional daily uses of vision.

● Partial participation in all activities is not always in the best interest of the visually impaired child's self-esteem. It is important that the child be able to participate fully and compete with others in some activities, such as swimming, judo, and wrestling. Partially participating in highly visual activities all the time may not promote a child's competence and self-esteem.

The developmental model and the functional-skills model are not mutually exclusive. It is possible to work aspects of the functional-skills model into developmental instruction. The teacher should use caution, however, not to rely heavily on developmental checklists for assessment and instruction. These really should be used only as guides and should never limit a child's potential or the teacher's creativity.

Functional skills form a major component of learning for all children—a fact that becomes significantly important in light of the realization that young visually impaired children may not incidentally learn important social skills, appropriate interactions with peers during play, and many of the essential self-help skills.

Teachers of visually impaired students, O&M specialists, and infant specialists can help families develop intervention strategies to address these key areas. Such intervention plans should reflect the family's priorities and be easily implemented within the daily routine. A functional approach, in which skills are introduced and taught within the natural context of occurrence, may be incorporated into the instructional plan.

Visually impaired children who are secure in their socioemotional development, have positive play experiences, and participate in activities of daily living will be better prepared for future integration and independence. The value of providing specialized instruction and developing competencies and confidence in these areas cannot be overestimated.

Chapter 5

BEHAVIORAL FOCUS: DEVELOPING POSITIVE STRATEGIES FOR BEHAVIOR MANAGEMENT OF YOUNG BLIND AND VISUALLY IMPAIRED CHILDREN

CONTRIBUTOR

Patricia Taylor-Peters
Behavior Management

Young visually impaired children can learn appropriate behaviors in the home and at preschool. Inappropriate behaviors often arise from such legitimate feelings as boredom, anxiety, frustration, isolation, and anger. With sensitivity, home and school environments can be designed to reduce or eliminate some of these feelings associated with lack of vision. However, it is often necessary to help shape children's behaviors in order to make them more socially acceptable, in the present and the future, and to maximize their potential for developmental gains.

Family members and professionals who work with young visually impaired children need to develop tools and strategies for behavior management. Inappropriate behaviors may stifle the development of strong attachments and may alienate extended family members and friends from engaging in meaningful relationships with the child. By cooperatively designing a behavior plan, the early-interventionist can help the family gain a sense of control in reciprocal interactions with the child, reduce associated frustrations and negativity, and increase the day-to-day enjoyment of parenting.

When they are provided with structure and limits, children may feel more secure and thus more able to function competently in our achievement-oriented society. It is important to remember that negative behaviors should not be allowed to define the child; rather, they are symptomatic of underlying feelings and causes that should be acknowledged and explored. If inappropriate behaviors are identified, it may be necessary to develop a behavior management plan to address a specific child's needs. The behavior plan should be beneficial to the visually impaired child, the family, and involved professionals. Suggested steps for designing an individualized behavior management plan are outlined at the end of this chapter. Such a plan should be implemented by someone at home or at school who is designated the "behavior manager." This person is the key to a successful plan.

THE BEHAVIOR MANAGER

Six key points for successful behavior management focus primarily on the behavior manager:

- Know yourself. Know what triggers your emotional reactions; know what you react to negatively and positively; develop self-observation skills.
- Reward yourself throughout the process. If you are not cognizant of your own reinforcers and do not reinforce yourself, you are likely to become emotionally exhausted.
- Know what you want of the child and why. Many people have a tendency to rush in and apply various strategies before determining their reasons for wanting change.
- Look; hear; feel; *perceive*. If you are not constantly doing so, you will miss important information.
- Verify your perceptions. Ask for others' opinions about what you are observing. Look and listen again to ensure that your perceptions are accurate and not biased by your emotions.
- Never take something away without giving something back. If you expect a child to give up an inappropriate behavior, make sure that he or she has an acceptable behavior that is equally rewarding to replace it.

OBSERVATION AND MEASUREMENT

Observation, measurement, and reinforcement are the key components of behavior management and therefore are the basis of the behavior plan.

Observable Behavior

Behaviors that are designated to be changed or managed must be observable. Observable behaviors are measurable actions and are different from labels for behaviors, which are subjective. Examples of observable behaviors are hitting, smiling, crying, turning away, and closing the eyes. Examples of labels are angry, sad, happy, disruptive, shy, and miserable.

In addition to the identification of measurable, observable behaviors, the establishment of priorities for changing behaviors is essential. Behaviors that cause injury to the child (for example, head banging) or to others (for example, biting) are priority targets for change.

Recording Systems

Several recording systems help in the observation and measurement of behaviors. These include:

- Permanent product recording, which records the items produced by the child, such as classroom papers.
- Event recording, which records the number of times a discrete action (such as eye poking or hitting) occurs.
- Duration recording, which records the length of an event (such as a tantrum).
- Interval-time samples, which record events in three ways—as a partial sample (events that occur within a portion of a designated time period), as a whole sample (how many times specified behavior occurs during a designated period), and as a momentary sample (behavior that occurs at the time observed within a designated period; once each minute during a five-minute period, for instance).

Format of Observation

The ABC method of observation is most effective. ABC is a mnemonic for *a*ntecedent to the behavior, *b*ehavior that is to be observed, and *c*onsequences of the behavior. Each of these elements should be identified, observed, and recorded when developing a behavior management plan. It is most helpful to start by identifying and observing the behavior, then the antecedent and consequences that surround it. For instance, when a child cries, it is important to note what happened before the crying began (was there a loud noise, did someone leave the room, or was another person or animal harshly addressed, for example). The type and length of crying should also be noted. There may be a connection between an event and the crying behavior. It is equally important to observe what happens after the crying begins (is the child immediately picked up, has the noise stopped, and the like). Developing an approach to observing a behavior within the context of the surrounding actions and reactions is the first step to understanding the behavior.

REINFORCEMENT

Reinforcement theory essentially states that people do what they do because of what happens when they do it. Frequently one thinks of reinforcement as having a positive focus. However, reinforcement also involves the concept of competing behaviors. Competing behaviors refer to actions that are incompatible with one another (for instance, a competing behavior for hand biting might be playing with a desirable toy that the child cannot play with at the same time he or she bites).

Reinforcement is anything that increases behavior. Reinforcement can be achieved either by giving or removing something. Positive reinforcement increases behavior because something is given (for example, the infant increases eating behaviors when soft music is played). Negative reinforcement increases behavior because something negative is removed; negative reinforcement is not punishment (for example, the infant increases eating behaviors when loud music is turned off). Punishment decreases or eliminates a behavior (for example, the child who is throwing food decreases the behavior in subsequent feedings because the parent turned off the child's favorite music).

To be effective, reinforcement should be immediate and consistent. When selecting reinforcers, it is beneficial to try to match them with an appropriate behavior the child already likes. Consider for example, that many young visually impaired children find enjoyment in movement activities, music or auditory stimulation, and edible and social reinforcers. It is important to individualize the reinforcers to the preferences of a particular child. Although it may not be easy to find reinforcers for some children who seem to be apathetic, there is always something to which each child will respond. It is also important to vary reinforcers. For very young children, it is often appropriate to start with tangible reinforcers—something that can be eaten or touched, such as a favorite snack or toy. Especially for the developmentally delayed student, however, it is important to match these tangible reinforcers with social reinforcers such as verbal praise and close physical proximity as soon as possible. It is also helpful to observe what happens immediately following high-rate behaviors, as such behaviors can be arrows pointing to the child's critical reinforcers. A critical reinforcer can be any event essential to a person's physical or psychological well-being.

TEACHING NEW BEHAVIORS

When attempting to teach new behaviors, it is important to identify the desired behavior rather than the problem area. Antecedents, those events occurring prior to the designated behavior, must be identified, as they can be manipulated to teach new behavior. In general, it is helpful to accept small increments of success rather than to require achievement of the entire goal at once.

Prompts are valuable tools in the teaching of behavior. They are anything that encourages the student to engage in the desired behavior. In order to be effective, prompts must be subtle rather than abrupt, and they must be gradually faded or discontinued. Modeling, physical guidance with gradual release, and backward chaining are examples of prompts. For example, the teacher may assist a young visually impaired boy in pulling his pants up to his thighs, with the child completing the task; the teacher then may only help pull up the pants knee high, requiring the child to do more of the task. This process continues until the child can complete the task independently. During prompting, an approximation of the task or desired behavior is reinforced rather than the entire goal behavior.

DEALING WITH MALADAPTIVE BEHAVIOR

Punishment used to stop a behavior is usually aversive. Aversive procedures are most often physically or psychologically intrusive. They inflict pain or discomfort and cause the child to avoid the person using the procedure and the general circumstances surrounding it. Aversive procedures teach the learner what to avoid, but they do not outline the steps toward appropriate behavior. Nonaversive procedures do not cause physiological or psychological discomfort, and most often they do teach appropriate behavior. So many negative associations and results are associated with punishment that it should be used sparingly in dealing with maladaptive behaviors. Punishment used unfairly usually breeds fear and resentment and does not promote learning.

In dealing with maladaptive behaviors, alternatives to punishment are used because they tend to be positive, increase self-esteem, and have educational value. Some alternatives are:

- Reinforcement of lower rates of the undesired behavior (for example, giving tokens for reduced eye-poking behavior for specified time intervals).
- Reinforcement of other behaviors and the ignoring of the undesirable behavior (for example, giving verbal praise for good posture while ignoring eye poking).
- Reinforcement of competing behaviors (for example, giving tokens for fine motor activities that involve or require both hands and therefore rule out eye poking).
- Extinction, or the ignoring of a behavior. It is important when choosing to use this alternative to be sure that the undesirable behavior can be tolerated (for example, attention-seeking behaviors that do not cause harm to the child or others, such as whining or screaming). This tolerance is important because usually the target behavior will initially increase before it decreases.
- Response cost, a consequence in which a negative response follows a demonstration of the undesirable behavior (for example, removing stickers from a preschooler's sticker card in response to his or her running around the room).
- Overcorrection, in which a child is required to continue to perform the designated behavior past the point he or she would normally choose. The child becomes bored with performing the behavior and gradually discontinues it. This method is more frequently used with older children (for example, a child who plays with his or her brailler at an inappropriate time is then to braille continuously until the teacher lets him or her stop).

TANTRUMS

A highly frustrating behavior exhibited by some visually impaired children is a tantrum. Tantrums may be viewed in the same manner as other, less disturbing undesirable behaviors.

In all likelihood, the young visually impaired child will have a tantrum for one of two reasons: either he or she is not getting something that is wanted or does not want to do something that is being asked. Tantrums are learned responses to situations and may continue as the child receives the expected response or desired outcome. The visually impaired child will learn new ways of behaving when he or she discovers that the tantrum does not pay off and that more acceptable, alternative behaviors will achieve the desired goal.

If one can ignore a tantrum because it is not destructive to property or person, then ignoring the behavior may extinguish it. If an ignoring strategy is used, one cannot respond verbally, in attitude, or in any way that gives attention to the tantrum. If this technique is implemented, the behavior will probably get worse before it gets better. It may increase in intensity, frequency, or duration until the child realizes that the tantrum is not receiving any attention or producing the desired effect.

It is important to try to teach children alternative, appropriate behaviors at calm times and to reinforce those appropriate behaviors. If attempts are made to take away a means of behaving that has been successful in the past, the child must be provided with new avenues of behavior that will be equally rewarding or successful. Children with a variety of impairments, including multiple impairments, are capable of learning strategies that do not incorporate crying and tantrums.

In the case of children who carry on a tantrum or cry for hours, it is best to consult with medical professionals regarding any physical implications or consequences before attempting to "ride out" an extended tantrum. If ignoring seems to have no effect after a week of full-blown tantrums, it may be time to try another approach.

Time-Out

Time-out is an alternative strategy for dealing with young children's tantrums. If a safe area of the home or preschool can be created where the child can go or be taken at the onset of a tantrum, placing the child in this area can serve as a means of removing all attention from the tantrum.

Using a timer set between 2 and 5 minutes is helpful in structuring the time-out. If the child is not quiet when the timer goes off, leave the child until he or she becomes quiet, saying, for example, "When you are quiet you may come out." If the child comes out before the timer goes off, take him or her back quietly and neutrally. Do not provide elaborate explanations or involve emotional reactions in the process.

Before implementing time-out procedures, consider whether or not you can leave the area quickly without a struggle or with a simple controlled removal procedure, for example, a two-hand hold (a hold that is secure enough to keep the child from escaping but gentle enough to cause no pain or discomfort). If you cannot, it is best not to attempt to remove the child. If the visually impaired child does not stay in the time-out area, holding the child very neutrally, with no words or emotions, can be a viable alternative for some children. Getting into a real tussle may prove counterproductive and suggests that something else should be tried. For the nonverbal or wheelchair-bound child, removing your physical presence may reduce tantrums.

Remember that time-out is only effective as a teaching strategy if you keep the time very short. Also consider that time-out may be a reinforcer to a child who prefers isolation from a group and therefore would be totally ineffective with such a child. Time-out should not be a form of locking the child away because of misbehavior; rather it is a way of creating a place and time for the child to calm down and to regain self-control.

Other Strategies

Tantrums can sometimes be eliminated by insisting that the child complete the activity he or she wants to avoid. If this alternative is used, physically move the child through the activity while limiting nagging words. Neutrally move the visually impaired child through the task. For example, if a child cries and falls to the floor because he or she does not want to put toys away, take the child by the hands to pick up the toys and guide him or her in putting them away. Say nothing. If there is too much scuffling while the child is having a tantrum, wait. When the child is quiet, do not ask for the toys to be picked up, especially if you notice that giving the verbal instruction triggers the tantrum. Just guide the child through the action physically.

If a child is prone to having tantrums in certain circumstances, it is helpful to identify them. Once identified, the situation can be arranged or changed so that the aggravating circumstance is lessened or eliminated. For example, if a young visually impaired child uses a tantrum to avoid bath time, begin with a less-threatening sponge bath. Initial attempts to have the child use the bathtub should be of relatively short duration. Favorite toys and music may be used to create a distraction for the child. Gradually involve the child in the bathing process by incorporating water play and body-part games. Surrounding the once unpleasant activity with pleasurable time and activities may make bathing more fun for everyone involved.

The following outline may be useful for family members and professionals who work closely with visually impaired children who have tantrums. This list for quick screening may help people gain insights into the cause-and-effect aspects of a child's tantrums:

I.   What does the tantrum look like?
    A.   Crying and screaming.
    B.   Throwing things.
    C.   Falling to the floor.
    D.   Running away.
    E.   Kicking and hitting.
    F.   Other _____ .

II. When does it occur?
    A.   When I say no.
    B.   When I take something away.
    C.   When I leave the child's sight.
    D.   When I'm giving another person attention.
    E.   When I ask the child to _____ .
    F.   When the child is tired.
    G.   During _____ activity.

III. How long does it last?
    A.   _____ minutes until I _____ .
                 (spank, give in, leave, and so on)
    B.   _____ minutes no matter what I do.

IV. How often does it occur?
    A.   Every day, _____ times.
            (number)
    B.   Several times a week.
    C.   Two or three times a month.
    D.   Only occasionally.

V.   Where does it occur?
    A.   _____ .
           (room/rooms)
    B.   In the front yard.
    C.   In the backyard.
    D.   In the classroom.
    E.   On the playground.

MANNERISMS

Many visually impaired children exhibit inappropriate mannerisms, including rocking, eye poking, head movements, and finger flicking. These behaviors may be symptomatic of a lack of stimulation and meaningful leisure-time activities.

Children who do not receive enough vestibular stimulation caused by movement of the fluid in the inner ear often engage in rocking or head movements in response to the basic physiological need for movement. Eye poking occurs with the discovery of visual sensations that may become a central focal point of enjoyment for the child, but the behavior may eventually cause structural damage to the eye. Finger flicking provides visual stimulation for children with low vision as the finger movement varies stimuli coming from a light source. Most of these behaviors eventually become habitual and provide a soothing distraction for the young visually impaired child.

Lack of vestibular stimulation can be remedied by providing appropriate movement activities, such as rocking in a rocking chair, swinging, rolling, spinning, bouncing, rolling on large gymnastic balls, and using a trampoline. These activities may encourage children to limit associated self-stimulatory behaviors.

Eye poking may be a symptom of a child's lack of stimulation.

Activities involving movement may help keep a child's hands occupied and reduce the need for self-stimulatory behaviors as well.

Eye poking, finger flicking, hand flapping, and other associated mannerisms are best reduced by substituting purposeful and equally motivating activities and behaviors. In cases in which those substitutions are not effective, more structured behavioral plans may be needed. Competing activities involving toy manipulation that occupies both hands may reduce the need for the mannerisms. Consistent positive and negative reinforcement in a behavior-modification program may also work. Verbal reminders alone rarely change these habitual behaviors, and ignoring the behaviors may accentuate the problem.

In general, young visually impaired children need to be actively involved in movement and social endeavors. Passivity and lack of movement often promote the increase in self-stimulating behaviors. Lack of vision inhibits the child's natural inclination to move out into the environment, explore, and initiate social interactions with others. This tendency may lead to increased egocentricity, which ultimately decreases the opportunities for the development of appropriate social behaviors.

EXTENDING APPROPRIATE BEHAVIORS

Any behavior management plan should include a method of incorporating the child's new behavior into a variety of settings. It is also essential to ensure that the new behaviors are not dependent on the presence of the instructor or the parent. The goal of a behavior management program is to promote the desired behavior independent of prompts or the presence of the adult who initiated the plan.

The following outline may be useful in designing an individualized behavior management program:

I. Select one distinct part of the day or activity on which to focus.
   A. Make sure it has a start and a finish.
   B. Keep in mind that it should be less than 30 minutes in most cases.
      1. If working on a project that is longer than 30 minutes, break it up into shorter periods.
      2. Note that longer activities can be broken up into:
         a. preparation

       b. participation

       c. cleanup

       d. summary (verbal review of the activity with the child).

C. Describe in narrative form (just as seen or heard) what is happening during the 30-minute period.

    1. What are the adults doing?

    2. What are other children doing?

    3. What is the child doing?

II. Decide on the detailed goal picture, the behavioral picture you would like to see.

A. Make it simple.

    1. There should be no more than three completely new behaviors for the child to learn within the goal picture.

    2. If the goal picture involves more than three new behaviors, break the picture into two parts. Implement one behavior management plan at a time for each part.

B. Make it relevant.

    1. The most beneficial goals are those that have functional implications.

    2. The goals should help the young child succeed in other areas.

III. Form a baseline.

A. Analyze the goal picture and list each of the behaviors.

B. Observe the child.

    1. See what the child does for each behavior.

    2. Notice what others do in relation to the child for each behavior.

C. Have a behavior specialist help with data collection.

    1. Frequency.

    2. Duration.

    3. Event recording.

IV. Design an intervention.

A. Decide what needs to be changed in order to achieve the goal picture.

B. Determine what needs to be taught.

C. Analyze how behavioral change and growth can be ensured and reinforced.

    1. Analyze this issue for the child's behavior.

    2. Analyze this issue for the adult's behavior.

V. Create a plan that will help the goal picture become generalized among different settings and people.

An organized and preplanned behavior system is more successful than a spontaneous, haphazard approach. Underestimating the capabilities of young visually impaired and multiply impaired children to develop appropriate behaviors limits both the expectations for them and the implementation of individualized behavior plans. The development of appropriate behaviors is critical for all children, for appropriate behavior promotes opportunities for continuing positive social and learning experiences.

Chapter 6

MOVEMENT FOCUS: ORIENTATION AND MOBILITY FOR YOUNG BLIND AND VISUALLY IMPAIRED CHILDREN

CONTRIBUTORS

Tanni L. Anthony
Definitions, Roles, and Assessment
Body Image and Spatial Relationships

Diane L. Fazzi
Environmental Considerations
Basic Skills
Mobility Devices

Jessica S. Lampert
Gross Motor Development

Rona L. Pogrund
Environmental Awareness
Basic Skills
Mobility Devices
Canes for Preschoolers

The area of orientation and mobility (O&M), with its emphasis on movement, actually encompasses all developmental areas. For the young child who lacks visual input, movement through the environment may not occur naturally. Sight is a motivator for movement, and through movement young children learn about the world. Through the process of moving, young visually impaired children are able to interact with the environment and develop conceptual understanding that leads to growth in all other areas of development.

EXPANDED DEFINITIONS AND GENERAL GOALS

The traditional definitions of O&M as found in the literature are, "Orientation is the process of using the remaining senses to establish one's position in the environment," and "Mobility is the capacity, facility, and readiness to move" (Hill & Ponder, 1976). The definitions are expanded and simplified when the focus is on early childhood. Orientation is the cognitive component of purposeful movement. Purposeful movement is defined as an intentional ambulation for a desired outcome. The goal is for the child to travel, in whatever mode possible for his or her development and physical ability.

The traditional components of O&M training used for adults and older children do not encompass the broad range of skills and developmental areas necessary to meet the movement needs of the young visually impaired child. The broadened definition of O&M for preschool blind children described by Hill, Rosen, Correa, and Langley (1984) included the following areas:

1. Motor development (gross and fine)
2. Concept development (spatial and environmental)
3. Environmental awareness
4. Community awareness
5. Working with the family and other school personnel
6. Formal orientation skills
   a. sensory skill development, including vision
   b. body image
   c. methods of establishing and maintaining alignment (trailing, squaring off, and so on)
   d. systematic search patterns
   e. measurement (time, distance, size, and so on)
   f. navigation and travel skills (use of landmarks, turns, soliciting assistance, route travel, and so on)
7. Formal mobility skills
   a. sighted guide skills
   b. protective techniques (forearm protective technique and lower-body protective technique)
   c. cane skills (indoor and outdoor).

Further information on these components can be found in the Peabody Preschool O&M Project (Hill, 1988), the first available example of a preschool O&M screening and formal curriculum.

The expanded definitions take into account the developmental elements that are the tools of independent travel. It is important to view early intervention O&M as a process that begins at birth. Sequences leading to independent goal-oriented travel are, for orientation: understanding one's body and how it moves, differentiating one's body from the immediate environment, understanding the world beyond one's body and reach, and understanding spatial and movement relationships; and for mobility: development and integration of reflexes, development of control over one's body, and development of goal-directed movement.

The goals of an early intervention O&M program are safe, independent, efficient, and motorically refined travel. The latter goal addresses the need for the child to demonstrate optimal skills in movement.

ROLE OF THE O&M SPECIALIST

An O&M specialist who has infant or preschool children in his or her caseload is faced with the following general responsibilities:

- Contributing as a member of the educational team, and as such, as a participant in the team-assessment process of the child. Other team members include the child's parents and professionals such as doctors, therapists, and educators.
- Providing developmentally appropriate goals and objectives for the educational plan. The O&M specialist is in an optimal position to demonstrate how developmental skills tie in with long-term O&M goals. For example, early auditory localization skills will ultimately assist the child in decoding the direction of street traffic.
- Developing and implementing educational activities for working with the child and the family. These activities should be tied in with the child's other programmatic needs. An example might be practicing mobility skills for learning the route to the bathroom while the child is simultaneously working on the goal of independent toileting.
- Analyzing the child's travel environments for safety factors and possible modifications. Another part of this task is to encourage the family to expose the child to a full spectrum of environments within their local community.
- Training, as necessary and possible, the other educational service providers of the child's program. This task might involve training in the use of specialized equipment or specialized skills for consistent follow-through.

In an educational setting, the O&M specialist is part of a team that consists of parents, child, teacher of the visually impaired, classroom or homebound teacher, and possibly other school personnel, including occupational or physical therapists, psychologists, and nurses, depending on the child's needs. Hill, Olson, Burke, and Smith (1989) state: "Optimum delivery of O&M services to visually impaired infants is provided through a coordinated team approach" (p. 54). Each member has specific expertise that is shared with the others. For instance, O&M specialists bring to the team a great deal of training in addressing needs directly related to visual impairment, and skill in presenting information about the environment, concepts, and movement techniques in easily understandable ways. Occupational therapists (OTs) and physical therapists (PTs) have skill and knowledge in the evaluation and treatment of developmental, orthopedic, and other physical problems that may affect the child's ability to achieve new skills. The effectiveness of any team depends on mutual understanding of each other's roles and abilities. In this respect the O&M specialist may initially have to educate other team members about the profession of O&M and become knowledgeable about other disciplines him- or herself.

As a team member, the O&M specialist must write goals and objectives for the child with whom he or she is working. These goals and objectives should be written to reflect functional skills. For instance, though a long-term goal of "completion of the Hill Performance Test of Selected Positional Concepts (Hill, 1984) with 100% accuracy" may reflect an understanding of the concepts included on the test in a testing situation, an objective that focuses on function would be, "When helping to put away his toys, Sam will respond accurately to directions that involve the spatial concepts of 'in front' and 'behind' on 4 out of 5 trials." In this way both the child's role (or expected activities) and the functional focus of instruction are addressed, and asking the child to

A visually impaired child may not need orientation and mobility (O&M) services at every point in his or her life. These visually impaired preschoolers are able to participate in activities with their sighted classmates without O&M training.

"place the ball in front" is an instructional strategy to meet the functional objective. Focusing on function may help all team members coordinate services in a defined way. All visually impaired children should be assessed by a qualified O&M specialist to identify their needs and reassessed to determine whether their needs have changed and if O&M services are needed.

Not all visually impaired children in all settings will need O&M services at all times. For instance, a student who is able to engage successfully in the same activities as his or her peers and whose present O&M needs are met might not need as much as one with the same diagnosis or visual condition but who is not keeping up with peers, is unsafe or hesitant in movement, or disoriented in the environment at home. The young child's expected activities at school (if applicable) and in relevant community settings should be addressed. Discussions with family and professionals involved with the child, review of available records, and direct observation are primary information-gathering methods. More formal assessment methods may be appropriate for some children and some skill areas. Information should be the basis for goals and objectives.

IDENTIFICATION OF NEEDS

Identification of the need for an early intervention O&M program begins with an assessment of the child and family. Information is gathered via interviewing the parents and directly observing and interacting with the child. An assessment and subsequent report should include background information, clinical impressions, a summary, and recommendations. The section on background information should include specific, pertinent information such as the child's current medications, diagnoses, and involvement in other educational and therapeutic programs. The clinical impressions section should consist of the names and brief backgrounds of the assessment techniques or instruments utilized, child-specific behavioral notes (for example, how the child was feeling or acting during the assessment process), and an environmental analysis of the assessment site. The summary of assessment results, including the child's functional vision, should be clearly written and understandable to families and involved professionals. The final section should list any recommendations for further testing, as well as specific programming suggestions.

A general developmental assessment yields considerable information pertinent to an early intervention O&M program. Not all this information must be assessed by the O&M specialist but can be obtained from other professionals in an interdisciplinary or transdisciplinary style (for further discussion of these styles, see the following chapter). In addition to overall developmental information, the O&M specialist should be concerned with the child's level of functional vision and auditory, tactile, and specific mobility skills. Finally, the specialist should consider the natural environmental opportunities presented to the child within the conditions of the assessment and their possible influence on the child's observed performance.

In addition to assessment or information gathering relating to the child's specific mobility skills, information should be collected on his or her general developmental functioning in the following areas because of the reasons described:

- *Sensory skills.* Knowing the status of the child's functional vision, hearing, and tactile development will provide information about the influences of lighting and noise, potential need for prescriptive devices, and the kind of teaching style that is suitable.
- *Cognition.* It is important to understand how a child processes information about the world and his or her level of problem-solving competence. Body image and time, space, and object-interaction concepts are included in this area. Orientation concepts are grounded in these early cognitive areas.
- *Fine motor development.* Prehension (grasping) patterns and general upper-extremity strength are building blocks for protective responses and techniques, trailing, cane use, and the like.
- *Gross motor development.* In addition to such developmental milestones as rolling and crawling, the child's "quality of movement" should be analyzed. This variable is important for the child's balance capabilities and quality of gait.
- *Receptive language and communication.* Understanding the child's level of language provides a guideline for how instruction should be presented to the child.
- *Self-help.* Activities of daily living may incorporate the use of functional routes (routes necessary for active participation in daily routines) for the child to practice. A route based on a need related to such an activity might be one used to travel to the high chair for mealtime.
- *Socioemotional development.* Social situations may be motivating for travel. It is

important to know if a child is responsive to praise or is reinforced by peer interaction in order to carry out route planning and determine style of instruction.

BODY IMAGE AND SPATIAL RELATIONSHIPS

Two important areas that are part of the foundation of O&M programming are body imagery and spatial relationships. Body image has long been recognized as the foundation of O&M concept development. Concepts of spatial relationships are tightly interwoven with the development of body imagery. The two cannot be fully separated. Similarities, however, are obvious as the sequences in the development of the child's sense of spatial relationships and body image are compared.

Cratty (1964) suggested that external space affecting a child's movement cannot be understood until the child is able to organize internal space. The sequence that O&M programming has followed in work with visually impaired children has traditionally been the identification of body parts, planes, movement, laterality (knowing one's own left- and right- sidedness), and, finally, directionality (the ability to differentiate between another person's left and right and to judge the position of objects in the environment relative to one's own body) (Cratty & Sams, 1968). Although this is an appropriate sequence, it can be limiting if the development of body image is to be fully addressed. A proposed sequence that includes the aforementioned components and encourages programming from infancy follows. The six levels should not be viewed in isolation but as a general guideline of what typically occurs from step to step. Children may cross over to a new area before fully developing skills in another area.

1. *Awareness of touch; movement by the whole body.* The infant begins to understand the layout of his or her body during the first months of being touched, carried, and positioned. Proprioceptive (sensitivity to the position of the joints, which gives postural information), kinesthetic (awareness of body movement or motion), and tactile (awareness of touching or being touched) input are primary modes of assisting the infant with building body awareness. Infant massage and bathing are excellent ways to provide this type of input.

2. *Awareness of body parts through movement.* Activities such as hand watching, clasping hands in midline, and moving feet to mouth are examples of this level of awareness of body image. The child begins to understand how his or her body is connected from top to bottom by moving his or her own body parts. As the process unfolds, the child begins to "map" proximal (parts of the body near the trunk) space and begins to learn about the immediate space around the body.

3. *Identification of body parts.* Body-part identification is typically assessed through the cuing of a series of rote responses, such as "Where's your _____?" Children learn the identification of parts of the body best when the body parts are involved in motivating activities. Play involving the fingers or parts of the body is ideal for the preschool child; coactive bathing, in which the parent uses hand-over-hand movement with the child to explore body parts while bathing, may be a more basic activity for a toddler or infant. While naming body parts and playing "tickle" games may be motivating and stimulating for both family members and the visually impaired

infant, many body-identification activities can be incorporated into functional routines for the preschool-aged child. "Put your arm through the sleeve" involves more purpose than a request like "Show me your arm." "Blow your nose with the tissue" is more relevant than simply requesting a child to "Touch your nose." More elaborate play activities that incorporate body-part identification and movement may promote socialization, self-confidence, and increased dramatic play.

4. *Identification of body planes.* Body-plane identification includes the understanding of one's body from the perspectives of top to bottom, side to side, and front to back. Internally, it may not include the child's labeling of the body planes. Activities that involve body planes are ideal for reinforcing the understanding of this concept. Putting on hats, shoes, and mittens or having a back rub are examples of such activities.

5. *Understanding of the relationship of body parts and body planes to movement (laterality and, later, directionality).* At this level the child comprehends that there is a plane that could make an imaginary division in the body from left to right, front to back, and top to bottom. The sequence of development of this process of organization is understanding of size and place, development of bilaterality, development of colaterality (relating to pairs of limbs), and differentiation of the halves of the body. Many mobility skills can be taught at this stage. The child may be developmentally ready to utilize a posture from a protective technique in an appropriate situation. He or she may be more able to respond consistently to a landmark or travel cue. Language is especially important at this stage. Concrete terms should be used when asking the child to move his or her body in a certain way. An understanding of the relationship of self to object and of spatial relationships grows out of this phase of skill development.

6. *Identification of self in relationship to objects and space.* At this stage, young children develop a greater cause-and-effect understanding. They may begin to move to familiar objects in the environment. Routes can be utilized to travel to desired locations, persons, or objects. The severely visually impaired child may initially need some degree of prompting or physical assistance in completing these types of tasks.

The process of developing the concepts involved in spatial relationships can be defined as the process of developing an awareness of one's body and where it is in relation to its surroundings, other objects, and the environment. Space can be analyzed as topical, projective, and euclidean. Topical space involves understanding the relationships of objects from a proximal to distal (body parts away from the trunk) perspective. The stage at which topical space is understood can be paralleled with the earlier phases of the development of body image, in which the infant begins to build "a body map" and "a near-space map." Projective space expands the concept of space from the isolated viewpoint of one's body. The child can separate space from a relationship of "where it is from me" to "by another point of reference." The euclidean level of spatial relations is complex and includes concepts such as distance and time measurements. These aspects of spatial relations are less relevant when working with the very young visually impaired child; as the child becomes older and more mobile, distance and time concepts are more important. For example, the preschool-aged blind child might begin to estimate when it is time to move toward the wall to trail and locate his or her classroom door.

A brief listing of the proposed sequence in which a child develops basic spatial-relationship concepts is as follows:

1. *Mapping of the immediate body (comparable with the first level of the development of body image).* At this stage, the infant is not aware of which parts are being touched or moved but knows only that there is a tactile sensation or motion of the body.

2. *Mapping of proximal space (comparable to the second level of the development of body image).* The child begins to search for items at near range, first those touching the body and then those within reach of the body. The use of a defined space is especially important at this early level because it assists the child in setting internal parameters concerning where he or she is within a particular environment. Objects should initially be connected to a stable site, such as to the child, the crib, or a table or tray where the child is situated. Later, the objects can be randomly placed by the child for discovery and interaction.

3. *Mapping of distal space.* At this level the child understands sound cues within his or her environment, is able to recognize landmarks within the environment, and moves with goal-oriented intention (for example, rolling toward a vocal parent). The child should have the experience of moving to a sound cue. If an infant hears the dishwasher from across the room and shows an interest in the sound, it would be beneficial to take him or her to the source of the sound. The child can then experience the dishwasher as the sound's source and the spatial aspects of the machine's location within the room.

4. *Mapping of near-range object-to-object relations.* The child begins to use objects together, understanding such concepts as play with toys with lids, organization of food in bowls or on a plate, use of tools to obtain objects, and the meaning of more complex search patterns.

5. *Mapping of body-to-objects relationships.* The child expands his or her understanding of space and learns prepositional concepts, body and movement games, negotiation of barriers, use of push toys or a cane, more complex search patterns, travel on routes to put away or retrieve familiar items, and trailing skills.

6. *Mapping of size and shape relationships.* In this phase, the child learns to use functional objects in varying sizes and shaped container toys. The understanding of seriation also occurs. Body games that require the child to be "small," "tall," "wide," and so on facilitate an understanding of size relationships.

7. *Mapping of part-to-whole relationships.* Use of puzzles, use of a part of an item or room, and recognition of landmarks through partial touch are skills demonstrated at this level.

As with the phases of the development of body image, the seven phases of the understanding of spatial relationships should not be viewed as strictly sequential.

Once the child progresses beyond the second phase, there is no linear model. Some components of various phases may be learned simultaneously.

GROSS MOTOR DEVELOPMENT

Gross motor development serves as the foundation for mobility skills in the young visually impaired child. These early movement experiences facilitate the development of muscle tone, balance, strength, coordination, and stamina (Cratty, 1971). All these elements lead to control of the child's body for safer, more efficient, and more graceful movement. Without vision as a motivator of movement, many visually impaired children lag in the areas of gross motor and sensorimotor development. These lags can significantly affect future performance in regard to mobility, and thus the visually impaired child needs structured early intervention in these areas.

The teaching and acquisition of O&M skills for very young children are closely linked with the child's total development (Coley, 1978). Although it is not usually the role of the O&M specialist to determine a child's developmental level, the specialist should be familiar with normal sequences of motor maturation and the achievement of milestones so that appropriate expectations are maintained and necessary referrals to other disciplines may be made when developmental deficits are suspected.

Several developmental checklists and inventories are available commercially. When referring to these checklists, it is important to be aware that there are typical differences in the rate at which children acquire the skills listed. Checklists should only be used as guidelines. Table 1 offers an overview, compiled from Gesell and Armatruda (1974), of typical milestones in gross motor development for the sighted child.

Sensory Integration

Current approaches to working with young visually impaired children emphasize the quality of a child's movement and the relation of sensory information to movement. Developmental checklists may help the O&M specialist establish a baseline of the child's performance or identify areas of possible deficit, but they do not in general provide information on how a child accomplishes a task or the presence or absence of problems with movement.

The sensory-integration approach is based on the concept that the gathering and processing of sensory information are the foundation of one's ability to deal effectively with the environment. It involves all the senses and emphasizes the tactile, vestibular, and proprioceptive systems (Banos, 1971).

The tactile system helps interpret sensations of touch. Information may be used for protection or for discrimination. Pain, light touch, and temperature are some of the sensations one experiences through the tactile system. Combined with other sensory information, tactile information helps one be aware of the body and how it moves through space.

The vestibular system provides information that helps one maintain balance, feel comfortable with changing one's position, and make postural adjustments to maintain an upright position. Its receptors respond to the pull of gravity, help one recognize at what speed and in what direction movement is occurring, and—when combined with

Table 1. Usual Sequence of Gross Motor Development for Sighted Children

Age at Which Behavior Develops	Examples of Behavior Demonstrated
0-4 weeks	When child lies on back, head is usually to the side and child's posture is asymmetrical.
1-2 months	When child is pulled to sitting position by the arms or shoulders, child's head tends to fall back.
3-5 months	When child lies on back, child's posture is symmetrical; by 4 months, hands come together at midline; child looks from hand to object; child begins rising up on forearms in prone position; by 5 months, child puts both hands on bottle.
6-7 months	Child transfers object from hand to hand; can sit briefly leaning forward on hands for support; by 6 months, Asymmetrical Tonic Neck Reflex (ATNR) (i.e., when child's head turns, limbs on the face side extend and limbs on the skull side flex; ATNR is the basis for visually directed reaching) is integrated.
10 months	Child sits unsupported; creeps; can go from sitting to prone position; pulls up to stand.
11–12 months	Child can pivot in sitting position; walks with one hand held.
18 months	Child walks alone steadily; uses pull toys; can seat self in chair.
21 months	Child walks down stairs with hand held; walks up stairs holding rail.
24 months	Child runs; can kick a ball on request.
30 months	Child jumps with both feet off the floor.
3 years	Child stands on one foot momentarily; pedals a tricycle; alternates feet when walking up stairs.

input from other senses—enable one to recognize whether it is the body or the environment that is moving.

The proprioceptive system provides information about one's body position; it figures in the ability to make automatic postural adjustments, in reflex reactions, and in the repetition of movements.

Interplay among the tactile, proprioceptive, and vestibular senses is important in developing an accurate understanding of the body (body awareness). Kinesthesia, an internal awareness of the body as it moves through space, develops from this communication (Heiniger & Randolph, 1981).

Recognizing that sensory information can have an effect on movement is important for the O&M specialist. It is possible that the specialist may more effectively teach skills through the use of many senses. An example may be the teaching of the forearm protective technique. Rather than simply positioning the child's arm and asking the child to repeat the position, the specialist may combine tactile and proprioceptive input by asking the child to "act like a statue" after he or she is positioned, while the instructor offers resistance to the movement of the child's arm.

An awareness of how sensation affects movement and the ability to interact with the environment will also assist the O&M specialist in determining when a referral to a professional in another discipline, such as an OT or PT, is necessary. For instance, a child who has difficulty discriminating textures, avoids contact with many tactile activities (contact with others, fingerpainting, gluing, and so on), or seems to find these threatening may be demonstrating signs of tactile defensiveness. Tactile defensiveness is the tendency to react negatively and emotionally to sensations of touch (Ayres, 1979). However, not every child who dislikes playing with fingerpaint or trailing walls or who seeks to avoid these activities is exhibiting defensiveness. It should be kept in mind that some standard preschool activities such as fingerpainting or gluing (glue may dry on the fingers) may interfere with the child's ability to use his or her fingers for gathering other information, and the child may object to the activity on that basis. In addition, the existence of normal preferences for and dislikes of activities among children should be acknowledged. A qualified therapist may help determine the presence of tactile defensiveness and suggest activities appropriate for the child.

A child who has difficulty relating his or her body to space, who seems to have an inaccurate body concept, and who has difficulty understanding and functionally using spatial movement concepts such as "in front," "behind," "under," and "over" may be demonstrating signs of poor kinesthesia. Although it is not within the realm of O&M to diagnose problems in this area, a referral to an OT or PT may be made on the basis of general behavioral observations and those specific to the individual child (Tyler & Chandler, 1978).

An OT can also be helpful in analyzing how to develop an individualized plan for a child, incorporating a variety of sensory inputs. The O&M specialist should make sure that the OT fully understands the skill or technique to be taught so appropriate methods and adaptations are developed.

When making a referral, the O&M specialist should be aware of the eligibility requirements of the agency or department to which he or she is referring the child. Sometimes frustrations develop when an O&M specialist feels a child needs therapy but finds the child is not eligible to receive the service. Knowledge of the conditions under which a child is eligible for service in various settings, and making referrals appropriately based on this information, may make the therapist more effective. In an educational setting, the more specific the O&M specialist can be in stating a concern, and the better able to relate the concern to the child's educational objectives, the better the therapist will be able to address the concern. The specialist should state the problem, describe how it interferes with functioning in the educational program, and ask for what is necessary. For instance, a description such as "Child withdraws from tactile activities" is probably not as helpful as the following: "Joe pulls away from any new textures and tactile games. This behavior interferes with the objective of exploring objects and space systematically, since he will not touch unfamiliar objects; with trailing, since he avoids contact with surfaces; and with participation in classroom activities. Can you provide suggestions?"

Motor Patterns of Visually Impaired Children

Visually impaired children commonly exhibit problems in movement or differences from the movement of children with unimpaired vision. Developmental lags (achieving milestones later than expected); problems in sensory processing, proximal stability (stabilizing one body part so another can move freely and functionally), and dealing with changes in position and use of atypical movement patterns usually associated with low postural tone have been noted in visually impaired children by several authors (Brown & Bour, 1986; Hill et al., 1989; Jan, Robinson, Scott, & Kinnis, 1975).

It may be helpful for the O&M specialist to communicate to others working with the blind child that blindness itself is not usually the cause of movement problems, although there may be a decreased internal or external motivation for movement that accompanies blindness. In general, blind children achieve static skills (those necessary to maintain stationary postures or positions) at the same rate as their sighted peers. Lags become noticeable in the achievement of transitional (moving from one position or place to another) movement. A blind child may require motivation from sources other than vision to lift his or her head and engage in a variety of movements or activities.

It has been noted that blind and visually impaired infants prefer a consistency in position and that they resist, or become fussy with, positional changes. For instance, many blind infants object to being placed on their stomachs. Although it is tempting to give in to this preference, it is important to remember that all positions provide experience necessary for the child's overall or global development. A variety of early experiences with movement can be developed with consultation from an OT or PT.

Blind infants also may tend not to initiate midline play and may require encouragement to do so. Placing a baby's hands on the bottle or breast during feeding and "motoring through" hand and finger play may increase the child's use of hands in the middle area of the body. By crossing the midline of the body, the child is able to integrate the left and right sides of the body and thereby increases overall functioning. This ability also enhances the performance of many mobility skills later on.

Reaching is another area that often requires intervention. Because seeing an object is a primary motivator for reaching, the child may need to be offered other reasons for attempting to reach for items not in contact with his or her body. Toys that make sounds are often suggested as motivators for reaching, but Kastein (1980) points out that in early infancy, the child does not yet understand that the sound represents the toy. Auditory toys alone may be ineffective in promoting reaching. For a more effective approach, sound may be combined with hand-over-hand activities in which the child is assisted to reach toward an object after it has been touched and been moved slightly away.

It is not uncommon for blind infants to skip the crawling stage of motor development. In some children, the avoidance of crawling may be related to the presence of low muscle tone and to the decreased ability to stabilize the neck and shoulder girdles. If there are no physical reasons for a child's avoidance of crawling or failure to crawl, the explanation may be that he or she receives negative reinforcement from bumping into objects in the environment in attempting to move headfirst without a warning system for avoiding obstacles. The pooled expertise of an O&M specialist knowledgeable about typical motor development in blind children and that of an OT or PT can identify the cause jointly. The O&M specialist can address atypical patterns of movement frequently observed in young visually impaired children from the standpoint of their possible relation to skills and vision. For instance, if a visually impaired 3 year old is often noted to maintain a head-tilt position to the side, back, or forward, the O&M specialist can determine if this is caused by an effort to control nystagmus or to deal with a functional field loss. A PT or OT should be involved to address the motor components that might be involved (poor head control, for instance) if a motor deficit is suspected.

Some of the more common movement and postural characteristics observed in blind and visually impaired children include maintaining the head forward and down or back; holding shoulders rounded forward, elevated, or retracted; using a wide base for sitting (spreading legs far apart for balance), standing, and walking; moving awkwardly from one position to another (moving in straight planes rather than incorporating rotation into movement patterns); and using a variety of gait patterns that differ from those of sighted children of similar ages (Brown & Bour, 1986).

Many of the atypical patterns used by visually impaired children are associated with low postural tone and compensate for lack of proximal stability. Although many of these compensations limit the movement of the body part the child wishes to stabilize and allow completion of specific tasks, they also tend to limit other normal functional body movements. True stability serves as a base for movement; compensation often limits movement (Bobath, 1974). If it is suspected that a child is using compensatory patterns or if the child is observed to use atypical movement patterns, the involvement of an OT or PT should be considered. It is not usually the role of the O&M specialist to remediate motor deficits (poor head control, poor balance, poor stability, and so on), although these areas are often addressed in the course of skill development. Working with therapists in various disciplines, the O&M specialist may structure lessons to address these issues effectively.

Strategies for Promoting Motor Development

The O&M specialist may incorporate a variety of developmental areas, and normal movement can be promoted by adapting typical O&M strategies. Placement of materials, structuring of activities to provide a variety of movement experiences, and modification of standard techniques are all important areas of consideration (Brown & Bour, 1986). Suggestions to facilitate motor development in the young visually impaired child include the following:

• Provide the infant with a variety of movement and positional experiences. Short, comfortable experiences may be more easily tolerated at first than 10-15 minute sessions. Tolerance can gradually be extended from a few seconds to greater periods of time.
• To encourage midline orientation of the hands and visual attention, use a pat-

terned cover on the infant's bottle. High-contrast patterns are best. Encourage the infant to hold the bottle during feeding.

- To orient the child to forward space and movement, it is helpful to work in front of the child rather than always from behind.

- To promote body awareness, concept development, and visual skills, while the child is on his or her tummy, place toys in front to either side. Encourage the child to shift his or her weight onto one arm and reach for the toy with the other.

- With the child sitting on the floor or straddling on a small bolster (with supervision only), place a set of items (such as blocks) on one side and empty containers on the other. Have the child take one item at a time and place it in an empty container. This activity addresses the O&M goals of concept development (empty/full, in/out, in front, beside, behind, turn, up/down, and so on). Other O&M areas addressed are visual skills, body awareness, and systematic search. Consider placement of containers to work on specific skills and concepts.

- To promote body awareness, concept development, independent movement, and route travel, use a scooterboard in a variety of ways. Have the child push or pull him- or herself across the room, follow a visual or tactile path, or hold a Hula Hoop while the specialist holds the other side, with the child indicating the speed and direction. Have the child go through an obstacle course.

- Scooterboards can be used with various positions (sitting; using legs to propel; sitting cross-legged and propelling with hands or being pulled; lying on back). Never use a scooterboard without providing much (preferably hands-on) supervision, and always check with a therapist before initiating scooterboard activities.

- Encourage the child to cruise for short distances holding on to a variety of surfaces at varying heights. For incentive and to add purpose to the activity, place a favorite toy or food a short distance from the child and have him or her cruise to locate it.

- Place a tactile marker or a favorite motivating toy or other object at the child's place at a table and have the child cruise (eventually trail) to locate it. O&M areas addressed include independent movement, beginning use of basic skills, and beginning use of landmarks. The marker may be visual for the child who has vision.

- To promote body awareness, social skills, and concept development, try playing robot or ballerina by balancing a beanbag or book on the child's head. Have the child try to keep the chin level as he or she sits or walks while balancing the book. Be aware of atypical posturing, and discontinue this activity if any is noted until checking with a PT or OT for ideas.

In cases in which children are receiving physical or occupational therapy, or in which there is any motor-development concern, a PT or OT should be consulted regarding the appropriateness of any of the activities listed above for intervention purposes. Every student has unique needs, and general suggestions such as those listed cannot take the place of a planned individualized program.

In organizing activities and lessons, it sometimes helps to define spatial boundaries with a blanket or carpet square, for instance. In addition, although it is sometimes easy to focus on learning a skill, in general the skill should not be removed from its functional realm. Developmental status should also always be kept in mind. For example, it makes sense that a child should be able to stabilize his or her shoulder and trunk before using forearm protective technique, to avoid promoting atypical movement patterns.

Parents, therapists, O&M specialists, and others can work together to promote normal movement experiences for the child. The goal of any O&M program is to maximize a child's ability to interact safely and efficiently with the environment. By working as a team, all involved can ensure success in the child's gross motor development.

ENVIRONMENTAL AWARENESS

Through encouraged exploration and interaction with the environment in both structured and unstructured formats, young visually impaired children develop an awareness of their environment. This awareness is the first step in creating motivation for the visually impaired infant, toddler, or preschooler to move. It also assists the child in making sense of the world, which in turn facilitates the development of orientation skills as the child develops. It is the role of families and professionals to provide experiences in the home, school, and community that will expand this awareness.

Home

Young children spend the majority of their time at home. Therefore the home environment is the logical place in which to provide the child a good initial opportunity for learning many environmental concepts. Families may have opportunities within the daily routine to teach concepts related to body image, as well as positional and functional concepts, which are the "foundations of environmental awareness" (Hill et al., 1989). For example, the young blind child in the scooting stage quickly learns to avoid the family pet's dish when he or she learns that the dish is located next to the refrigerator, that the dish holds the pet's food, and that the rule is to keep "hands off." Knowing this series of conceptual relationships builds images in the young child's mind, which assist in the development of understanding the connection between the child and elements of the environment.

Making sure the child has opportunities to explore various parts of the house in a systematic manner helps the child piece together the environment in a meaningful way. As the child begins moving by crawling or cruising, providing verbal descriptions of the household environment is beneficial. It is useful to talk in terms of relationships such as, "You're touching the couch, which is next to the kitchen door." Environmental awareness starts the process of "landmarking," in which the child designates certain objects as landmarks and which is a very important orientation skill for the blind child. Making sure the child is not just familiar with one or two rooms of the house means that the whole concept of "house" is eventually understood. Noting tactile differences (carpeted, tiled, wooden floors, and the like) and auditory cues (such as toilets flushing, garbage disposals grinding, radios playing, and wind chimes ringing) heightens the child's environmental awareness through the senses, which also serves as a foundation for future orientation skills.

School

The preschool environment can also be a rich learning experience for the young blind child. It is important that the child's awareness of school not be limited to the routes from the bus or car to the entrance to his or her classroom and to the bathroom and play area and back. Does the child know that there are many rooms off the hallway on both sides? Does the child know that there are stairs leading to a second floor at the end of the hallway? Does the child know that there is a kitchen with appliances and counters and shelves, where lunch is prepared, and that meals do not magically appear on a tray from nowhere? Has the child had the opportunity to explore the entire play area in a systematic manner, or does he or she only know about a favorite swing? Are the relationships between each of the parts of the school and the functions of each understood?

The visually impaired child deserves to know about the total school environment so that his or her conceptual knowledge increases and "gestalts" of the world are built. Learning certain travel routes to follow by rote sometimes has its functional purpose and may be necessary, but the blind child's world must be expanded with the help of trained professionals if generalized travel is to be a future goal. For some severely cog-

By using small-scale models and props, this orientation and mobility specialist is helping a visually impaired preschooler become more familiar with the playground layout at his school.

nitively delayed children or children with spatial orientation problems, rote route travel may be the primary travel method in learning needed functional routes. The child with multiple impairments, however, also deserves the opportunity to explore his or her environment in a more generalized sense, even if the child is unable to transfer orientation strategies and concepts to larger environments.

Community

Sighted children learn about their community outside the home and school by going to the bank, the store, the post office, the fast-food restaurant, and so on with their parents from an early age and observing the environments around them. They see the colors and shapes, the uniforms the workers wear, the buildings inside and out, and all the many features and activities that teach them about each community environment they visit. They also learn a tremendous amount about the outside world from the visual media. Television and movies open up many unknown worlds to the sighted preschooler.

Blind children do not have these vast opportunities to take in the world visually and expand their conceptual understandings. They are only aware of the places and activities in the community to which someone has exposed them and carefully explained what is happening. Tactile, auditory, olfactory, and visual (if available) exploration accompanied by meaningful verbal descriptions provides the only way the visually impaired child can make sense of the world around him or her. Otherwise, the child has only bits and pieces of a very fragmented world, which leave often confusing and inaccurate images of the environment.

Outings into the community should be an important component of the young visually impaired child's O&M program. Parents and professionals can create opportunities for the child to experience pet stores, grocery stores, airports, restaurants, gas stations, post offices, taxis, office buildings with elevators and escalators, bus rides, bowling alleys, and the like. Each new experience in the community at an early age adds another piece to the conceptual puzzle. It is not unusual to find an older congenitally blind child, ready to learn street-crossing skills, whose understanding of "intersection" is limited to the tactile and proprioceptive feedback received under his or her feet while walking with a sighted guide down a flat, smooth surface, stepping down a dropoff, walking over a rougher surface, and stepping up again. He or she may also have been aware of a variety of confusing surrounding sounds. He or she may not, however, have been aware of the parkway to the side, the driveways passed, the houses to the other side, the way the curb runs, the gutter, the wheelchair ramp at the corner, and the like. He or she also may not have any idea how the two streets crossed to form an intersection and may not know about the other two corners, the systematic way the traffic flows, or the traffic light overhead. How can this child be expected to cross the street safely and remain oriented, given such large conceptual gaps?

Parents and professionals have an important responsibility in teaching young blind children about their community and the world at large. Verbal descriptions alone are not enough, or the "verbal unreality of the blind" described by Cutsforth (1951) may occur, in which the blind child grows up with intricate verbal descriptions of the world but with no true understanding of the environment and little ability to interact functionally with it. For the child with multiple impairments or the very young child with little or no receptive language, nonverbal methods of communicating about the environment must be employed. Lots of hand-over-hand touching and exploring, along with physical prompts and motoring that are paired with labels and verbal descriptions, are necessary to bridge the communication gap. Early, meaningful instruction in environmental awareness is the only way to create future success in this area.

Awareness of all these environmental concepts can begin at a very early age, as parents and professionals expose the child to the outside world and take the time to explain this complex environment carefully. It is not possible to teach everything about the environment to the preschool-aged visually impaired child, but whatever he or she learns about early on will provide that much more of a head start when the child competes in a sighted world and applies O&M skills in the future.

ENVIRONMENTAL CONSIDERATIONS

In determining environmental considerations for young visually impaired children, the O&M specialist must make suggestions that will enhance the accessibility of the surroundings, improve the motivation for efficiency of early movement, and ensure the safety and security that are essential to confident movement. The O&M specialist may be asked to make such suggestions in the home, in the yard, at school, or on the playground. Environmental considerations are important for visually impaired infants, toddlers, and preschoolers, as they may serve to inhibit or to enhance independent movement.

Considerations for Infants

Sleeping, feeding, and bathing areas for visually impaired infants may be adapted to provide a stimulating environment for waking hours. An interesting and accessible environment can promote initial exploratory behaviors that provide the foundations for early movement. Ideas and practical suggestions relating to adaptations for visual, auditory, and tactile development are highlighted in Chapters 2 and 3. Many of those suggestions are relevant here as well, due to the interconnectedness of various aspects of development in young children. Visual, auditory, and tactile development represents a few of the components from which the motivation to move stems.

The essential considerations for such adaptations should be the safety of the visually impaired infant and the general interest level of the environment to an infant with a vision loss. Safety issues are similar to those for sighted infants. Although they are well known, they need to be kept in mind and include:

- Pillows, stuffed animals, and the like should not be given to small infants, who may smother themselves as they try to explore the objects or wriggle in their cribs.
- Objects given to infants should be large enough so that they cannot be swallowed as the child mouths them.
- Larger toys and objects should not have smaller, removable parts that may find their way into babies' mouths.

- Visually impaired infants should not be left unattended in infant walkers, swings, and so on.
- Safety straps should be used on the changing table and high chair to avoid dangerous falls, even if the infant is to be there only a few minutes.

For more detailed information on infant safety, there are many manuals and resources available from health centers, infant safety classes, libraries, and bookstores.

Suggestions for increasing the interest level of the visually impaired child's environment with the intention of prompting reaching and exploratory behaviors to promote movement may include:

- Natural lighting can be maximized for visually impaired infants during waking hours (for example, by opening drapes and curtains or placing the crib or infant seat in a well-lighted area). Optimal lighting may help the child with low vision to see contrasts, shapes, shadows, objects, and faces more clearly.
- High-contrast (black-and-white) mobiles can be placed within grasp of the visually impaired infant to promote reaching, a sense of causality, and awareness of the outside environment.
- Securely mounted shiny objects, Christmas lights, and mirrors can be used to form mobiles or mounted against contrasting backgrounds (for example, by the changing table) to provide structured visual activities that promote reaching, head movements, visual tracking, and exploration.
- High contrast among bathtub, soap, and bathtime toys may promote vision use by infants during bathing.
- During daytime feedings, optimum natural lighting can be used to facilitate increased infant-caregiver attachment. Under optimum lighting conditions, visually impaired infants may be better able to see the silhouette, shape, or details of the caregiver's face.
- Musical items may be used as mobiles for blind infants. (It is important to remember that while eye-hand coordination typically develops in the sighted infant at approximately 4–6 months, ear-hand coordination does not typically appear until approximately the 10–12 month developmental period. Although auditory stimulation is of great importance to the blind or visually impaired infant, expectations must realistically consider the delay that many visually impaired infants will experience in this area.)
- Adaptations can be made in the home that may heighten the child's awareness of the environment. For example, a soft-sounding wind chime hung in a doorway may alert the blind infant to people's entrance into a room. This type of warning may also give the child a greater sense of control and security. In addition, it may lead to attending behaviors such as head turning, reaching, and babbling sounds which strengthen the child's interaction with the environment. These kinds of skills and involvements with the environment are some of the important precursors to purposeful movement.

Considerations for Toddlers

Environmental considerations for visually impaired toddlers may be slightly more complex. Not only must the child's surroundings provide security, motivation for movement, and opportunities for exploration, but arrangements must also take into account the toddler's need for support during cruising and other attempts at first steps and walking.

Safety. Adults should be concerned about objects with which the toddler may unknowingly or unsuspectingly come into contact while crawling or cruising. Corner protectors are commercially available for tables, shelves, and countertops to protect children from injuries caused by falling onto or running into sharp furniture edges. Objects at head level are of particular concern for young visually impaired children and their families. Care should be taken to ensure that tablecloths are not hanging over the table edges where the child can pull on them and spill hot food, knock over candles, and so on. Electrical socket plug covers are available, as are electric-cord shorteners, which keep cords out of children's reach and limit entanglement and tripping.

Motivation. Many sighted toddlers begin their first movements in response to a desire to reach an interesting object or person. That same motivation needs to be present for visually impaired toddlers. As visually impaired toddlers learn cause-and-effect concepts, they will receive enjoyment from reaching favorite toys or objects and being able to manipulate them. As they expand on their social interactions, visually impaired toddlers will be reinforced to move through their meaningful contact with significant people in their lives.

Some of these motivating factors, which seem to occur as a matter of course, need to be well thought out for the visually impaired toddler. Discovering likes and dislikes and incorporating that information into programming may foster positive early movement experiences for the visually impaired toddler. Those early experiences help to expand the young child's environment and broaden the physical and social interactions contained within the child's experiences.

Support. Toddlers often use furniture to gain support for upright movement. Sighted toddlers have the advantage of being able to plan visually a trail of support for getting where they want to go. The visually impaired toddler, cruising along the edge of a couch, may be at a loss as to where to go next. Furniture may be arranged to provide support for the visually impaired toddler in a logical sequence that allows for movement to meaningful locations. Once the furniture is arranged to meet some of the toddler's needs, as well as the needs of the family, it should be left in place as much as possible. This physical stability allows the child to begin using basic mental mapping and orientation skills. Initially, stability is important to the formation of foundations in orientation processing and application. In later childhood, however, it will be important for visually impaired students to have opportunities to experience and adapt to changes in the physical environment. If changes in furniture are necessary, it is important to reorient the young child by giving verbal descriptions and by physically guiding the child to the new furniture placements to ensure that he or she understands the changed spatial relationships.

Considerations for Preschoolers

The preschool visually impaired child who is fully ambulatory requires a whole new set of considerations. The environment should be secured for the young, inexperienced traveler, but it can also become a tool for use in the development of initial travel-orientation skills.

Safety. In response to similar concerns expressed regarding safety for the toddler, the home and school environment for the visually impaired preschool child should be examined for head-level obstacles; knee- and shin-level obstacles; cords, wires, and throw rugs that may cause tripping or slippage; and stairs and other dropoffs that may catch the young child off guard. Commercially available corner and edge protectors can significantly diminish the danger of bumping into obstacles. Rubber housings for loose cords and wires can eliminate entanglement of the curious youngster. Various types of plastic and rubber mats are available for placement under throw rugs. These mats significantly reduce slippage and turned-up corners on area rugs. Secure safety gates can be used to block off stairways in the home to allow the visually impaired child to move more freely during playtime.

For the preschool child who has low vision, the use of color and contrast may be used to increase safety in the home or at school.

- A dark area rug on top of a light-colored carpet (or vice versa) can alert the visually impaired child to the location of a coffee table or other piece of furniture.
- A dark-colored cloth or drape can help the young child with low vision detect a glass tabletop or other piece of furniture with glass, which would otherwise be difficult to see.
- Contrasting place mats and dishes can reduce the number of accidental spills and breakage.
- Planned color choices for cupboards and furniture or brightly colored decorations can reduce collisions for visually impaired children in their preschool classroom.

Travel and Orientation. As the visually impaired child's ability to move increases, the child's environment expands and its personal relevance increases. Certain considerations can help to create home and school environments that are both accessible and meaningful to the young visually impaired child.

For example, fenced-in play yards provide ample opportunities for safe and independent movement. If outdoor toys are routinely stored in an accessible area, the environment then possesses a natural motivation for the young child to move when it is the child's responsibility to retrieve and return his or her toys.

In addition, walkways and surface changes (grass to gravel, cement to dirt, hedges to open areas, carpet to linoleum, and the like) can provide both indoor and outdoor landmarks and easily followed routes to favorite areas in the home, yard, or school. These types of ready-made or adapted environmental characteristics can assist the visually impaired child in orientation processing and decrease the child's dependence on adults for movement.

Environmental considerations for the young visually impaired child and for the family who wants to be actively involved in promoting their child's desires and abilities in regard to movement should not be overlooked. Although some considerations may require more effort, time, and expense than classroom teachers or families are able to expend, most adaptations will require minimal investment of time and money. The O&M specialist should plan to devote ample time to observing the child indoors and outdoors and in both the home and school. Careful observations of movement and inter-action patterns should determine which environmental considerations are priorities to be addressed. Ongoing observations will help update modifications to keep in step with the changing needs of the visually impaired child as he or she matures and develops.

BASIC SKILLS

Instruction in basic skills is typically an integral part of most O&M programs for young visually impaired children. Basic skills include, but are not limited to, sighted guide technique, protective techniques, and trailing. The instructional techniques, usage, and potential benefits of these basic skills may differ from the techniques and benefits commonly associated with older children and adult populations.

Sighted Guide Technique

As young visually impaired children start to walk, they can begin to benefit from the use of the sighted guide technique. In using this technique, the blind person holds on to the sighted person's arm and walks a half step behind and to the side of the guide, following the guide's body movements. Rather than always holding the young blind

The guide's middle and index fingers are held by the child in this modified sighted guide grasp.

child's hand and pulling him or her through unknown space, adults can use a modified sighted guide grasp with the child, in which the child holds the guide's index finger or hand in such a way as to obtain a sense of control while walking to the side or
behind the guide. As the child grows older, the sighted guide grasp may move closer
to the guide's elbow (from the finger to the hand to the wrist to the forearm). The
sighted guide technique is a safer, more efficient way to lead a blind child than is walking side by side and holding the child's hand. For example, a young child using modified sighted guide is more likely to avoid people and obstacles because the child can
interpret the body movements of the guide.

Sighted guide instruction should not be limited to the blind child and the immediate family. Instruction should be extended to other adults, such as the preschool
teacher, child care worker, and teaching assistant, and extended family and friends
who may come in contact with the child. In addition, peers and playmates should be
instructed in the proper use of the technique. Eventually, the visually impaired child
will be required to take a more active role in instructing those around him or her in the
proper techniques for sighted guide. This training should begin as early as possible to
avoid the passivity often demonstrated by many young blind children, who are often
pulled about by their well-meaning peers.

Protective Techniques

When young blind children move through their home, school, and play environments
independently, there may often be unexpected obstacles. Protective techniques are one
defense against bodily contact with some of these hazards. When executed properly,
forearm protective technique, in which the arm is bent at the elbow and placed across
the body at shoulder height parallel to the floor with the palm outward, will guard
young children from head- and chest-level obstacles. Similarly, lower-body protective
technique, in which the arm is extended downward and diagonally across the body at
the hip area with the palm toward the body, guards against contacting obstacles at
waist to upper-leg level. When used with consistency, however, these techniques may
become physically fatiguing for the young child. Selective use of protective techniques
in unfamiliar areas, in familiar areas where certain obstacles are known to exist, or
when sighted persons give verbal warnings of potential hazards, is more appropriate
and realistic than continual nondiscriminatory usage.

Protective techniques are limited in the amount of protection they provide, particularly in unfamiliar areas. Even in cases of perfect execution of these techniques, individuals may contact hazards with the knees, shins, ankles, and toes. It takes a refined traveler to be able to adjust forearm protection for obstacles of differing height. The less
sophisticated traveler, who is unable to distinguish the height of head-level obstacles, is
at risk for upper-head-level injuries. Because of the high level of muscle tone and motor
coordination required for proper use of protective techniques, young children commonly exhibit inexact technique and are prone to unexpected collisions. The number of
these collisions may discourage the young blind child from using the techniques daily.

Although protective techniques are valuable skills to be used in selected travel situations, the reality is that, in isolation, these skills have significant limitations. If a

young blind child's only sources of protection for independent movement are forearm and lower-body protective techniques, the risks of movement may ultimately outweigh the motivation to explore the environment. These skills are most beneficial when taught and used in conjunction with the long cane—a more reliable, independent protective device.

Trailing

The basic skill of trailing, in which the traveler extends the arm at a 45-degree angle in front and to the side of the body to follow a surface with the hand, has multiple functions. It can be used as a method of alignment, as a method of gathering information, and as a form of protection during movement. As with protective techniques, the usefulness of trailing may be limited and may depend on the accuracy and consistency of the arm position and the concentration of the traveler. Modifications in trailing for young blind children involve varying arm and hand positions, depending on the particulars of the environment and the child's motoric capabilities.

Cruising, commonly used by young toddlers for balance and support prior to walking independently, is a preliminary form of trailing that should be encouraged. Typically, children will progress from holding on to a table or couch edge with two hands to holding a furniture edge with just one hand to trailing the edge of a surface. Cruising is important because it facilitates movement, exploration, and independence for the young blind child.

For young blind children who are able to walk independently, trailing a surface edge or wall may provide a general sense of security as they move through the environment. Trailing technique can be enhanced when taught and used in conjunction with the long cane. The cane not only provides extra needed lower-body protection for the young traveler, but it also allows the

This little girl is using modified trailing technique to move around her school independently.

trailing hand more freedom of movement for exploration of the trailed surface.

Traditionally, a large amount of time has been devoted to teaching basic skills to young visually impaired children, and traditionally, young visually impaired children

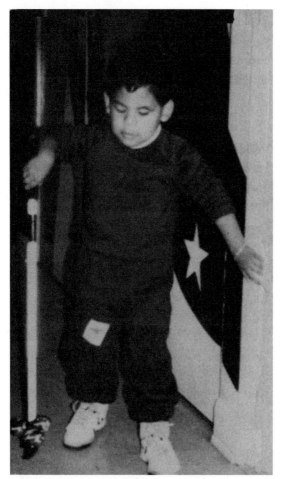

Trailing technique used in conjunction with a long cane is manageable and useful for this 2-1/2-year-old boy. His AFB Kiddy Cane has been adapted for him through the addition of jingling bells near the tip to increase weight and help prompt him to move the cane.

rarely incorporate these skills into their daily routines. Basic skills too often become associated only with O&M lessons. Young children need to understand the purpose behind the use of such techniques. When blind children internalize the cause-and-effect relationship between the use of techniques and safe and efficient movement, they are more likely to be motivated to use their skills. For children with poor muscle tone or with physical impairments, protective techniques and trailing may be very difficult to master because they require shoulder-girdle strength and arm-and-wrist rotation. For children with any physical impairments, consultation with a PT should occur prior to instruction in these motorically difficult skills.

It is important to teach and practice basic skills in a functional context. This approach helps children associate the skills with their everyday use. For example, sighted guide may be practiced with a child's preschool-aged peer as the class moves from the classroom to the playground. Forearm protective technique should be taught in an area with actual head-level objects the child could safely contact while using the proper technique (for example, air conditioners, open cabinet doors, and dining room tables). Trailing should be taught and practiced along a wall that is typically traveled during the child's regular routine (classroom to bathroom, kitchen to the family room at home, cubby to the classroom door, and so on). Associating basic use of skills with their functional purposes helps children, families, and teachers to understand, accept, reinforce, and utilize these techniques in an appropriate context.

MOBILITY DEVICES

No one disagrees about the importance of movement for young visually impaired children. It is through movement that young children learn about the world, develop muscle tone and coordination, and become actively engaged with other people and their surroundings. There are a variety of viewpoints, however, regarding the most appropriate devices, techniques, and teaching strategies to best promote this movement. Mobility devices may fall into several broad categories, including infant appliances (such as walkers), toys, adaptive devices, and long canes.

These devices may have selective use with individual children at various developmental stages, with individual children who have various motor capabilities, and with individual children as they interact in various social situations. In the long-term perspective, most blind children will ultimately utilize the long cane for independent travel. With this goal in mind, and with those goals of promoting movement, exploration, autonomy, socialization, and improved gait and posture, decisions regarding the appropriateness of specific mobility devices should be incorporated into the O&M program. The determination of the most appropriate mobility device for any individual child should be made by a certified O&M specialist with input from parents and other teachers and from a PT as well when there is any question about the device's impact on the child's balance, posture, gait, or motor development.

Infant Appliances

Early childhood specialists, special educators, PTs, parents, physicians, and manufacturers are in discord over the possible pros and cons of such infant appliances as jumpers and infant walkers. Although these appliances may provide some early movement experiences for young children, they should be used only with extreme caution. Jumpers are appliances that are mounted in a door frame and have a canvas seat attached to coiled springs. Even when used with constant supervision, baby jumpers have been associated with sprained ankles, leg injuries, and detached retinas.

Infant walkers may act as a buffer between the child and the environment during the early movement stages. However, their use requires constant supervision by a responsible adult. Blind children in walkers may easily topple down dropoffs or stairs. Infant walkers may move very quickly along noncarpeted surfaces, causing collisions and spills, especially in movement over changing surfaces. The constant use of an infant walker may inhibit development of normal motor patterns and balance and may decrease opportunities for creeping and crawling (Clarke, 1988). Given the special motor development needs of young visually and multiply impaired children, it is essential for educators and families to consult with PTs regarding the appropriateness of any infant appliance.

Toys

As the young visually impaired child begins to stand, take first steps, cruise, and move through the environment, a variety of toys or objects may be used for support or may provide some degree of protection. Some toys and objects may be used in conjunction with a sighted person to provide initial movement experiences. These experiences, which still depend on the presence or assistance of a sighted person, may serve as transitions from sighted guide to independent movement as distances are extended between the guide and the child (Clarke, 1988). Examples include Hula Hoops, rubber rings, broom handles, or any object that is held by a sighted person as the blind child also holds it for support while walking.

When the child is ready to move more independently, toys such as beach balls, Hula Hoops, toy shopping carts, push toys with wheels, and toys that are ridden may be used for support or as bumpers for protection from collision with obstacles in the environment. Children may use some of these items to navigate in appropriate play situations.

Although some of these toys and objects may have a certain value for children in need of support for balance and for certain social situations, they also have inherent limitations. Some toys may not withstand the weight of a child in need of support, so care must be taken to ensure safety through adaptations (weighting toy shopping carts with sandbags or pushing them in reverse, for instance). Some of the items are bulky and provide more protection from the environment than is necessary (for example, pushing a large Hula Hoop may limit the areas accessible to the young child and may limit hands-on contact with the surroundings).

Using many of these toys may seem natural in a play setting for a young blind child, but the same toys may appear out of place in other settings. For example, a Hula Hoop used by a blind preschooler may be accepted on the play yard but may be totally unacceptable in the lunchroom. A toy shopping cart may be used appropriately on a route to collect milk from the kitchen at school but may be less appropriate to take routinely on the route to the bathroom. A beach ball may serve a useful purpose in the home as the young child pushes it to avoid collisions with furniture but would not be appropriate to use in a store or in the general community. If toys are used in a safe, functional, and socially appropriate manner, they may be useful for some visually impaired children in the early stages of walking. Using toys that are not safe, functional, or socially appropriate may serve to inhibit movement, decrease generalization of travel skills, and increase social isolation.

Adaptive Mobility Devices

Mobility devices may be adapted by O&M specialists or may be commercially available. Specialists have adapted more traditional mobility devices for young blind children, as well as for children with multiple impairments. Such adaptations may include long canes with dual handles (one for the child and one for the instructor to help motor techniques); canes with wheels, coasters, or gliders; and devices made of polyvinyl chloride (PVC) pipe with curved tips or tubed rollers and two-handed handlebar grip. Commercial devices such as the Push Pal™ have also been developed for early movement. Many of these adaptations have been designed to meet the individual needs of children who have motoric impairments and who are unable initially to utilize the traditional long cane. In most cases, these devices should be used as transitions to the long cane by shaping the skills necessary to use the cane. For children, multiply impaired or not, who are initially or eventually able to use the long cane, it is most beneficial to do so at an early age, as this is the mobility device the child will most likely use in the long term. It is also the device most likely to be accepted and understood in the larger community, as some of the adaptive devices may be confused with devices for physically impaired persons and may make the child look more "handicapped" than necessary. Clarke (1988) has developed a Checklist for Evaluating

Mobility Devices, which may serve as a useful guide when determining the most appropriate mobility device for an individual child.

USE OF CANES WITH PRESCHOOLERS

The sequence of skills currently used in O&M for children and adults was originally developed for adults. In accordance with this sequence, mastery of so-called "precane" skills, such as sighted guide, protective, and information-gathering techniques, and understanding of a variety of spatial and environmental concepts were required prior to the introduction of cane skills. Because of the prevalence of this philosophy, the introduction of cane skills was commonly delayed until a child was at least 8, 9, or 10 years of age and after the basic skills had been refined. Only recently have long canes been introduced to children as young as age 2. A term preferable to *precane skills* is *basic skills*, those basic to all travel, and not necessarily a prerequisite to use of a cane.

Traditional Arguments Against Early Cane Use

Several reasons have been used to support the delay of introduction of cane skills. These reasons, and responses to them, are presented in Table 2.

Late introduction of the cane may have long-range social, physical, and cognitive implications. These include:

● Development of inappropriate gait patterns (shuffling, taking small steps, slapping the feet) and postural positions (head down, stiffened movements) in response to moving in an uncertain environment and fearing a loss of balance.

Table 2. Arguments For and Against the Early Use of Canes

Traditional Arguments	Responses
Young children lack motor control and are not physically ready to be introduced to complex cane skills.	The cane does not necessarily have to be used in a complex way; the child may be taught to use the cane in a modified diagonal or constant-contact technique initially that does not require a great deal of motor coordination. Many basic skills (such as trailing and forearm protective technique) involve more complex motor skills than using a cane.
Young children do not need a cane in familiar areas.	Children need canes anywhere adults do; the general environment is too unstable and unpredictable to ensure safe travel.
Young children might hurt someone else with the cane; they are not mature enough to handle a cane safely.	A child can be taught to "handle" a cane; safety rules and responsibility can be taught, just as with any other potentially dangerous tool or toy.
Young children will develop bad cane habits, such as uncentered hand position, if a cane is introduced too early.	Cane skills are developmental; they can be refined as the child gains motor control (much as a child scribbles before he or she acquires the skill of writing).

- Development of fear of movement, with resulting passivity; protective techniques do not offer enough warning or protection against low obstacles and changes in terrain.
- Lack of exploration of the environment, leading to development of inaccurate and incomplete environmental concepts.
- Development of lack of confidence in the ability to control self and the environment; lack of autonomy leading to "learned helplessness."
- Possible difficulty in gaining acceptance of the cane by the family, the child, peers, and others when the cane is finally introduced.

There are several potential advantages to introducing the long cane early. These include:

- Increased freedom of movement..
- Increased ability to explore the environment, resulting in increased knowledge of the environment.
- Development of a more secure, natural gait and a more appropriate and relaxed posture.
- Increased stimulation of the vestibular system, resulting in a decreased need for self-stimulation.
- Increased self-confidence and autonomy as the child appears more competent to others.
- Early acceptance of the long cane by the child, family, peers, and others.

The long cane may also be helpful for some children with low vision. If the decreased vision interferes with movement and travel, the cane may be used for lower-body protection, as well as to help identify the child as a visually impaired person. Working with a cane enables the child to use existing vision to gather relevant information from the environment rather than having to keep the eyes on the ground constantly in fear of obstacles, dropoffs, and terrain changes.

Suggested Strategies and Techniques

The development of cane skills in young children is relatively slow compared with skill development in adults. Instruction involves shaping the skill and giving the child enough time to acquire it. It is also important to make learning to use a cane fun and a positive experience for the young child.

Cane Readiness. Mastery of many of the concepts, cognitive abilities, and motor skills previously considered necessary before introduction of the long cane are, in reality, not prerequisites. For the visually impaired child who has no other physical impairments, two motor abilities are key to success with the long cane: the ability to hold the cane in some fashion, and the ability to walk independently with adequate balance so as not to need the use of high- or medium-guard positions (in which the arms are bent up at $90°$ or $60°$ angles, respectively, for balance) or help from a person or balance device. If a young visually impaired child has additional physical impairments that preclude holding the cane or using it while maintaining an acceptable gait pattern, it is recommended that the O&M specialist consult with a PT.

Expressive language abilities are not a necessity in receiving instruction in cane travel. Modeling, nonverbal communication, physical prompting, and receptive touching (for example, interpreting a touch on the shoulder as a message to stop) are effective instructional tools for use with children who have limited receptive-language abilities.

Only a limited awareness of objects in the immediate environment is necessary for cane instruction. An understanding of object permanence, cause-and-effect relationships, and the function of the cane as a bumper can actually be facilitated through cane instruction and movement activities. Similarly, spatial concepts and environmental awareness can be promoted. For example, a visually impaired child does not need to be able to identify or locate specific body parts in order to use a long cane; the child only needs to be able to utilize functionally some of those body parts in order to be successful (Pogrund & Rosen, 1989).

Instructional Approaches. Suggested instructional considerations for the introduction of the long cane include the following:

- Safety rules should be taught, emphasizing that the tip of the cane initially stays on the ground at all times and that the cane stays in front at all times when the child is walking.

- Names of the parts of the cane should be taught in order to establish a common terminology if the child has sufficient language and cognitive ability.

- Methods of holding the cane while using a sighted guide should be taught, as this will be a frequently used skill for the young child as he or she goes to and from lessons and travels with friends, parents, and teachers.

- Use of the cane as a bumper and probe should be taught because the very young child will use the cane primarily for these purposes.

Young visually impaired children can be taught about canes and about appropriate safety rules as well. This little girl is learning the parts of the cane.

- Alternative techniques may be taught according to the child's needs and motor abilities and include modified diagonal technique with the cane arm relaxed at the child's side, modified diagonal technique used while trailing, constant-contact technique, and two-point-touch technique.

- Cane skills can be integrated into basic skills instruction and development of concepts, language skills, and body awareness, rather than be treated as an isolated instructional activity. For example, trailing the wall to locate a landmark can be taught in conjunction with diagonal cane technique; squaring off (putting one's back and heels against a flat surface to gain alignment) can be practiced while using the long cane in crossing a hallway; cane usage can facilitate the acquisition of environmental concepts through increased movement and exploration; and spatial concepts such as "down," "center," "back and forth," "across," "forward," and "front" are reflected in long cane instruction.

● Cane use should be incorporated into daily activities as soon as possible in order to provide many natural opportunities for practice.

● Family members, other children, and related professionals should receive in-service training before the young visually impaired child uses the cane in the given setting.

● The young child should have an assigned place to store the cane when it is not in use. Folding canes are usually best kept with the child's personal belongings in order to foster a child's sense of autonomy and responsibility.

General Suggestions. The following suggestions may be useful in working with young children:

● Marking the cane's grip with a paper clip and masking tape or with a piece of felt or using a specially designed grip with a finger ridge for young children helps the child know where to grasp the cane. The American Foundation for the Blind (see "Resources" for further information) has developed a "kiddy cane" with special features helpful to the young child.

● Initially, trailing the baseboard where the wall meets the floor with the tip of the cane can assist the young child in kinesthetically learning the diagonal position.

● Marshmallow, mushroom, and teardrop tips for canes are useful because they tend to glide over uneven surfaces more easily than do other tips, they are slightly heavier than other tips, and they provide additional cues for keeping the cane tip down.

● Hip holsters that can be attached

As he climbs these stairs, this little boy is demonstrating everyday use of the long cane at school.

to the child's belt or pants loop can serve as a convenient storage place for a folding cane not in use. (Cane holders are available from HandiWorks in Palmdale, CA.)

- Allowing the child to hold or periodically check his or her cane arm with his or her free arm may initially help the child maintain the cane arm in proper position.
- Correct terminology is important, but it is also helpful to pair the new term with something that makes sense to the child (for example, pairing *arc* with *sweep it back and forth*).

When working with young children, it is important not to try to work on everything at once. Learning to use the long cane should be a motivating experience for the child. With the development of O&M for infants and preschoolers, new information and ongoing research will be needed.

As the population served by O&M specialists changes to include more infants and preschoolers, the role of the specialist changes as well. The specialist's major responsibility continues to be the encouragement of optimal independence and the provision of motivation for a child with a vision loss to travel within a variety of environments. A responsibility of the field as a whole is to develop further and refine appropriate methodologies to achieve these goals. This effort will require more than a shift from the formal O&M techniques and applications to a developmentally appropriate approach. The latter will demand further research and collaboration within an early childhood spectrum of education for children with vision loss.

Chapter 7

TEAM FOCUS: NATIONAL TRENDS, SERVICES, AND ADVOCACY IN PROGRAMS FOR YOUNG BLIND AND VISUALLY IMPAIRED CHILDREN

CONTRIBUTORS

Diane L. Fazzi
Service Delivery

Alana M. Zambone
National Trends

Rona L. Pogrund
Teaming and Advocacy

Although early intervention services have been available for many years, new knowledge about the importance of the early years of a child's life and the role of the family has resulted in a significant expansion of these services, culminating in legislative support. On October 30, 1986, the amendments to the Education for All Handicapped Children Act (P.L. 94-142) (as of 1990 called the Individuals with Disabilities Act [IDEA]) were signed into law. This legislation, P.L. 99-457, while addressing a variety of educational services, has two major areas of impact: It extends special education services to include all children with disabilities from 3 through 21 years of age, and it provides strong incentives for states to offer services to eligible children from birth.

This emphasis on early education is not new. Original drafts of P.L. 94-142 contained provisions for early education. During the financial and political "refinements" of the subsequent drafts of this law, however, the age for eligibility was changed to 6 years because, in part, of a pervasive belief that mandated services would violate the family's right to full responsibility for the development of their young child. Thus, P.L. 94-142 only supported competitive distribution of discretionary funds for a limited number of demonstration projects serving young children, the Handicapped Children's Early Education Program (HCEEP). P.L. 99-457 redesigned the criteria for distribution of discretionary funds and made them available, on a noncompetitive basis, to all states and territories that chose to comply with the criteria. It is important to note that the criteria reflect the importance of the family in the young child's development, particularly in the requirements relating to interagency coordination with parent representation, the family's right to refuse services and protection of their rights of due process, and the Individualized Family Service Plan (IFSP). Passage of this law is the most significant indication of changing current trends in early education. The law has also had a major influence on every aspect of services.

CURRENT TRENDS IN SERVICE PROVISION

In an examination of legislation and practice in early education for children with visual impairments, several national trends emerge in the areas of research, service delivery, and personnel preparation.

As reflected in funding priorities, priorities in research have changed from developing new models, as in HCEEP projects, to the following:

- Evaluating current techniques, models, and combinations of models,
- Delivering services in new and different ways to varying target audiences in both rural and urban settings,
- Preventing developmental delays or secondary disabling conditions and enhancing development rather than emphasizing remediation or correction,
- Measuring the efficacy and efficiency of services in response to the call for greater accountability and the need for cost-efficient services.

Early education, particularly for children with visual impairments, has expanded dramatically, demanding increased and different services and redefinition of professional roles. These demands are reflected in changes in early childhood special education, including:

- Varying and flexible service models that include a variety of service options for families,
- Diagnostic, assessment, and intervention procedures focusing on identifying needs and strengths rather than on using developmental labels and categorization, and based on a more eclectic theoretical application incorporating developmental, functional-behavioral, and psychoeducational approaches,
- Mandated coordination and collaboration at the state and program administrative levels and transdisciplinary service delivery at the direct service level,
- Strong focus on the family as the intervention agent and emphasis on meeting family concerns as reflected in the IFSP. The IFSP, like the Individualized Education Plan (IEP), is to be developed and include goals and objectives based on assessment, as well as scheduled reevaluation.

Changes in personnel preparation are occurring in response to the needs created by changes in service delivery. These changes include:

- Increased emphasis on the early childhood special educator as a facilitator for the family, in combination with direct instruction of the child,
- Increased emphasis on the role of the teacher of visually impaired students in collaborative efforts,
- Increased emphasis on the use of a transdisciplinary approach as well as cross-categorical and multiple-role competencies,
- Increased efforts to define the parameters of specialty areas,
- Increased emphasis on skills required for team functioning and information sharing.

Several concerns have been engendered by P.L. 99-457 and the impact of current trends in regard to young visually impaired children. Visual impairment is not specifically mentioned in the legislation on the list of examples of eligible disabilities. This oversight is probably due to the legislation's strong emphasis on at-risk indicators and developmental delay. Professionals in the field of visual impairment are fully aware of the powerful effects of vision loss on development at an early age. However, vision specialists are not on the list of examples of professionals to be included on the service delivery team. Thus, needs related to visual impairment could be overlooked or inappropriately met, particularly for the child who does not have an apparent eye anomaly or who is not exhibiting significant developmental delay.

In addition, the law does not require that children be labeled or categorized in order to be eligible for early childhood services. This can cause problems for the population with visual impairments because (1) access to specialized materials is based on identification and labeling, (2) successful lobbying for a share of limited resources depends on an accurate child count, and (3) lack of a child count makes it difficult for school systems to plan for the specialized resources and personnel required by children with vision loss.

Special educators must become involved in the planning process at the state and local, as well as the programmatic, levels to ensure that young visually impaired children and their families have the specialized resources and intervention they require. Mobilizing and working with parents, including the involvement of organizations such as local affiliates of the National Association for Parents of the Visually Impaired (NAPVI), in this advocacy effort is one critical strategy (see "Resources" for the address). Educating others who serve young children with special needs about visual impairment and vision resources is also important to the effort to ensure that appropriate services are provided. Only through a true team effort will high-quality service delivery models be established for young visually impaired children and their families.

SERVICE DELIVERY

Included among the possible options in service delivery models for young visually impaired children and their families are the multidisciplinary, interdisciplinary, and transdisciplinary team approaches for serving individuals with special needs. Program options may also vary and may include center-based programming, home-based programming, and combination programs for young children and families. The most appropriate placements for young visually impaired children emphasize the meeting of all educational needs—those typical of other children of similar age and those particular to children with visual impairments. Class size, student-staff ratios, and professional preparation and competencies are all important considerations in making proper placement determinations. Open discussion and clear understanding of the professional roles of the teacher of visually impaired students, the orientation and mobility (O&M) specialist, and related staff and specialists help to ensure the appropriateness of services rendered to young visually impaired children and their families.

Team Models

No matter what service delivery model is used for young children, a team is always involved. Effective team functioning is critical to planning and providing a good educational program for the child. The use of a team in education has been advocated by those who are interested in the whole child and by those who feel that knowledge of the various aspects of the child must be integrated in order to help the child reach maximum potential. No one person can have all the necessary skills to meet all the child's needs.

Depending on the child's needs, the team of professionals working with a child with visual or multiple impairments may include, but not be limited to, any of the following:

- parent or primary caregiver
- special education teacher
- psychologist
- teacher of visually impaired students
- O&M specialist
- physical therapist (PT)
- occupational therapist (OT)
- speech therapist
- ophthalmologist
- optometrist
- adaptive physical education teacher
- nurse
- health care aide
- social worker
- parent advocate

Staff-to-student ratios are an important factor to consider when assessing appropriate programs for the individualized needs of young visually impaired children.

- instructional assistant
- regular education teacher.

Whenever teams work with a child, they may need to be alert to barriers that interfere with effective team functioning. Lack of communication can be the biggest barrier to effective functioning. This lack of communication often occurs during assessment, the writing of objectives, and IFSP or IEP meetings, as well as during implementation of the program. Members of the team may fail to communicate with each other on a regular basis, and specialists in one field may not have a clear appreciation of the skills another discipline wants to teach. Each discipline has its own jargon, and team members may not understand each other's terms. In addition, parents and professionals may meet very few times during the school year, so interaction between them may be superficial.

Lack of coordination and collaboration is another barrier to effective functioning. Assessments, planning, and program implementation are three areas in which this can be seen. Assessments are frequently not coordinated among team members and so may duplicate one another. Objectives may be written with no consideration of the priorities of other team members (for example, without consulting with the teacher of visually impaired students, an O&M specialist may plan to work on cane skills on a functional route to the lunch area; however, the teacher's primary focus might be on toileting, but the young child is not familiar with the route to the bathroom), and each team member may implement only his or her own program.

In addition, when team members have differing perceptions of a student's needs, the members may begin to feel that their professional judgment is being questioned. It is not uncommon for professionals to disagree about a child's need for academics rather than a socioemotional emphasis. When these differences are not dealt with professionally, discrepancies may lead to animosity among team members.

Follow-through is important to the workings of the team and the child's program. When team members do not follow through in providing services they have agreed to provide, trust is undermined. For example, teachers who agree to reinforce basic mobility skills in the classroom but do not follow through interfere with the student's progress and frustrate mobility specialists. Such behavior severely hampers team functioning.

Personality differences and other personal issues and dislikes, when allowed to dominate, can interfere with communication and team functioning. It is important to try to work past personal differences.

Finally, the issue of territoriality can be troublesome to teams. The feeling of needing to protect one's own area of expertise interferes with the team's efforts. This feeling often comes from insecurities about one's own professional abilities or distrust of another person's abilities. For example, an OT or PT who does not trust the abilities of an instructional assistant may not spend the necessary time training the assistant in positioning strategies. Range-of-motion activities may not be shared for fear that other teachers or assistants may overstep professional bounds. When one has confidence in one's expertise and trust in others, sharing and communication take place.

Three Primary Team Approaches

Regardless of the term used to describe the educational team, the purpose of the team is always the same. The team is established to provide the best overall educational programming for a particular child.

The three primary team models are (Perske & Smith, 1977) multidisciplinary, interdisciplinary, and transdisciplinary. The multidisciplinary team is traditional practice based on a medical model. The child is seen by a variety of specialists at different times, in sessions usually carried out away from the classroom or home. Professionals involved seldom communicate, collaborate, or make common agreements with each other about service delivery. The classroom teacher has little input regarding decisions about the child. Usually, the teacher or parent is a recipient of recommendations that are most frequently provided in writing and that may conflict among the various team members. This model often results in a very fragmented program.

The interdisciplinary model reduces fragmentation in programming. As a group, team members focus on one child's functioning, share assessment findings, and develop objectives together. The parents' and teacher's roles in this model are minimal, however. Team recommendations are often more ideal than practical because they are based on isolated views of the child.

In the transdisciplinary model, one or a few people are responsible for direct contact with the child. Usually the teacher or the parent is the primary service provider. The composition of the team depends on the child's needs. Role release, in which fixed roles are diminished, allows training and a particular specialty function to be carried out by more than one person. The specialist releases his or her role to the primary service provider. Direct care is handled by the persons closest to the child and those who work with the child most regularly, and team members offer consultative backup. The transdisciplinary approach has been defined as a deliberate pooling and exchange of information, knowledge, and skills, involving the crossing and recrossing of traditional boundaries by various team members (Hutchinson, 1974).

For a transdisciplinary team to work, three elements must be present: (1) joint team effort, in which a team performs aspects of the program together; (2) staff development approach, in which team members train one another; and (3) role release, in which various professionals teach one another to implement training procedures and skills that by tradition have been considered the sole responsibility of one individual.

Role release does not imply that the professional abdicates professional responsibility. Professional accountability is not relinquished. Team members remain accountable for what they teach and how well the skills are learned.

Role release refers to three levels of sharing (Lyon & Lyon, 1980):

- *General information*, in which knowledge of basic skills and practices is communicated (for example, the O&M specialist teaches related staff to utilize adapted sighted guide technique with young blind children).
- *Informational skills*, in which others are taught to make specific judgments or decisions about something that has been taught so a skill may be reinforced (for example, the OT shares information on a child's self-feeding ability so that the classroom

teacher may reinforce skills and hold consistent expectations of independence).

● *Performance competence,* in which others are trained to perform specific actions (for example, the PT trains a classroom aide in proper positioning and lifting procedures to use with a physically disabled, visually impaired child so that lifting and positioning can be done in the classroom without the therapist present).

Considerations for using role release include the student's needs, the expertise available on a team, logistical constraints, and legal ramifications (for example, certain medical procedures should only be performed by the appropriate specialist).

The transdisciplinary model is based on the belief that therapies should be incorporated continuously and naturally into the child's daily activities at school or at home. Skills taught in short episodes twice a week are probably not going to be integrated into the child's repertoire. For example, if O&M skills are only practiced when the O&M specialist comes to the preschool, the visually impaired child will most likely not incorporate the skills into his or her everyday activities in a meaningful way. If the classroom teacher and assistant are shown the appropriate skills and have the child utilize them, then the daily reinforcement will help the child functionally interpret the skills.

In this scenario, the program facilitator plays a key role. The facilitator may be any member of the educational team. This person has the responsibility of coordinating and integrating the delivery of the various services provided. The educational facilitator gathers information from a variety of resources and disciplines and incorporates it so that effective intervention is carried out. A good facilitator must have a sound working knowledge of all the disciplines, know the psychology of coordination and group dynamics, possess ample time and energy to complete necessary duties, be willing to serve as a team member, know how to bring parents effectively into the team, and have good group communication skills such as listening, negotiating, and exercising tact.

The transdisciplinary model initially seems more difficult to sustain than other models because it may be new and because participation in it seems to take more time. Once roles are assumed, however, it actually allows more students to be reached and is less time-consuming than traditional models. A well-run team makes significant contributions to the child's growth.

Program Options

Program options may vary for visually impaired infants, toddlers, and preschoolers according to individual needs, service availability, and funding constraints. Familiarity with programming possibilities can assist professionals and families in locating or providing appropriate services.

Center-based programs are available nationwide for young children with special needs. Not all center-based programs are alike, nor are they intended to be similar service delivery models. Some center-based programs are privately funded, while others must meet public agency guidelines. Programs may be generic in nature, working with young children who have a variety of special needs. Such agencies may or may not employ or contract for the services of professionals who have specialized training. For example, a generic program may hire a PT on a contractual basis to work with young children with motor difficulties or a teacher of the visually impaired to work with a young visually impaired child who may be enrolled in the program.

Disability-specific center-based programs provide another option for children with special needs and their families. Such programs are designed to meet the needs of children with specific, primary disabilities (for example, children who have orthopedic disabilities, hearing impairments, or visual impairments). Specialized programs should be staffed by professionals with specialized training or experience that qualifies them to work with the specific population.

Integration with nondisabled peers may be incorporated to varying degrees in center-based programs. Integration may occur at the school site or at a separate location. Children with disabilities may be placed with nondisabled peers, or an arrangement of reverse integration may bring nondisabled children into classrooms with children who have disabilities. Other opportunities for integration may occur within the community itself.

Parental involvement is another element of center-based programming for young disabled children that may vary greatly. Although some programs may mandate parental involvement as a requisite for a child's enrollment, other programs may not incorporate a caretaker component. The type of involvement may range from informal parent groups to actual hands-on work with the children.

Center-based programs for young disabled children vary greatly in structure and scope. Young visually impaired children and their families may or may not find a variety of center-based options, depending on the availability of programs in their area.

Home-based programs are another service delivery model for young children with special needs and their families. Home-based programming may incorporate direct service, consultation, or a combination of the two. Such services may be provided by any number of professionals, including a nurse, social worker, OT, PT, teacher of visually impaired students, O&M specialist, or early childhood special educator. Frequency of home visitations varies from monthly to weekly and may vary from program to program.

Other programs operate combination center-based and home-outreach service delivery in order to meet more diverse needs of the child and family. For example, parents may attend support group meetings at the center and receive direct service for their child at home. Some mothers of visually impaired infants attend "mommy and me" classes at a center and then receive home-monitoring support. In these combined models, some children and families may receive one or both forms of service, based on family and child need or program organization.

Most Appropriate Placement

Selecting the appropriate program model for the visually impaired infant, toddler, or preschooler can be challenging, to say the least. If a wide array of options is available, families must explore their own concerns, priorities, and resources in making appropriate determinations. Efficacy studies as to the effectiveness of different early childhood intervention models have been limited in scope. Especially in the area of visual impairment in infancy and early childhood, there are few definitive studies that might suggest which program models promote optimum child development, caretaker-infant attachment, and family support and involvement.

The Most Appropriate Placement (MAP) (Curry & Hatlen, 1988) for young visually impaired children considers both the developmental needs that the young child shares with nondisabled peers and the child's disability-specific needs. The MAP is the optimum choice for an individual child at any given time and may change periodically. For example, a young child who is developing braille readiness skills may need the intensity of specialized instruction in a preschool class designed for visually impaired children. That same child may be mainstreamed in a regular education academic program later in life once adequate braille skills are developed.

Proponents who believe that integration is the most desirable option for all children insist that integration with nondisabled peers is the main intent of the Least Restrictive Environment (LRE) clause of P.L. 94-142. The LRE for the visually impaired child is that placement deemed best to meet all the child's educational needs (Hatlen, 1990). Integration with sighted peers is one among many considerations when determining an appropriate placement for a young child with a visual impairment. Hatlen maintains that the most accurate interpretation of LRE is "the educational placement which least restricts the child's opportunity to learn" (p. 2). For many visually impaired children, early years spent in a separate specialized setting promote the learning of skills that will facilitate successful integration in later school years and in adult life in society. IEP and IFSP decision-making teams must make careful determinations based on individualized, comprehensive, unbiased assessments. A child's placement should reflect those assessed needs and the family's resources and realistic concerns.

Specially Trained Professionals

Visually impaired infants, toddlers, and preschoolers have many unique needs that are directly related to their disability. Incidental learning, which is primarily a function of vision in early childhood, is severely limited for the young visually impaired child. For this reason, visually impaired infants, toddlers, and preschoolers require the specialized services of teachers of visually impaired students and O&M specialists, who have specialized training that enables them to readily adapt curricula, utilize effective methodologies, modify the environment, and address the special needs of the population (Hatlen & Curry, 1987). Without specialized training in the area of visual impairment, generic special educators and early childhood specialists, who in all likelihood may have strong backgrounds and contributions to make in the area of general development, may not have the knowledge base or experience necessary to provide appropriate programming for young visually impaired children.

When investigating possible program options for young visually impaired children, the extent and quality of specially trained professional involvement should be thoroughly researched, including the availability, training, and backgrounds of relevant specialists and their experience with young children with visual impairments.

This involvement is a key element in meeting the unique needs of this low-incidence population.

Class Size

Class size and student-to-staff ratios are both important factors to consider in evaluating a center-based program's appropriateness for young visually impaired children. Totally blind youngsters require much one-on-one attention from staff because many activities must be done "hand-over-hand" for the child to gain maximum benefit and performance. Young blind children in general do not have the capabilities to learn casually and profit from other student and staff activities that occur beyond their reach. The auditory information received by these young children is inadequate in comparison to the visual input received by children of similar ages with other disabilities. Young students with low vision also require more individualized attention due to the limited, inconsistent, and sometimes inaccurate visual input they receive.

Smaller, more manageable class sizes are often more appropriate for visually impaired children. Based on state and national averages, class sizes for classes designed specifically for visually impaired infants or preschool-aged children with one teacher and one aide should range from 4 to 8 students. Kindergarten class sizes should range from 6 to 10 students (Hazekamp & Huebner, 1989). It is also important to consider that additional assistance from aides, related service staff, volunteers, or older students may be particularly beneficial during feeding, toileting, dressing, and field trips to the community.

It is equally important to consider caseload size of staff when selecting home-based programming for visually impaired infants or preschool-aged children. Large caseload size may be associated with a low frequency of direct service by qualified professionals. Based on state and national averages, a caseload range of 13 to 17 students should be considered an appropriate guideline (Hazekamp & Huebner, 1989).

In recommending or selecting a program for a young visually impaired child, it is important to consider the family's comfort. Families have differing life-styles and have differing economic, physical, and emotional supports and resources. They need to be comfortable with the philosophies and staffing of the child's program as well as with the more logistical aspects such as location, funding, scheduling, and family involvement. The family's comfort ensures a more positive parent-professional collaboration as well as a more positive outcome for the child.

PROFESSIONAL ROLES

In programs for young visually impaired children, the vision specialist or teacher of visually impaired students is a vital team member. The vision specialist is particularly qualified in the following areas:

- Providing help with programming decisions,
- Reviewing possible program options and placements,
- Completing specialized assessments, including a functional vision assessment,
- Adapting assessment materials and procedures for other professionals,

- Interpreting medical and functional eye reports for related professionals and families,
- Securing adaptive materials and equipment for educational purposes,
- Providing in-service training to preschool staff and students,
- Serving as case manager in coordinating related services,
- Delivering direct services to visually impaired children and their families in center-based or home-based programs,
- Providing consultation to families and related professionals on such matters as programming, placement, curricula, and direct service.

In providing direct service to young visually impaired children, vision specialists may address areas of child development on which vision loss has an impact. For visually impaired infants, particular emphasis may be placed on visual, auditory, tactile, olfactory, and kinesthetic sensory development. The teacher of the visually impaired may also be involved in providing enriching activities and environments that promote language development, play skills, and movement. Additionally, he or she provides direct support to families in areas of concern related to general caretaking (including feeding, diapering, bathing, and so on).

When working with visually impaired toddlers and preschoolers, the vision specialist's focus may be adjusted to include more structured aspects of development. Braille readiness is one of the structured educational components that is incorporated in the teacher's area of direct service. The preschool-aged blind child may be introduced to exercises that promote tactile sensitivity, page orientation, and tracking ability in regard to braille reading. Young children may also begin experiencing the use of braillewriters, learning correct finger placement, and developing necessary finger strength. The vision specialist might help the preschooler with low vision learn to use a magnifier for looking at letters and pictures and to develop page-orientation and line-tracking abilities.

Although auditory development is important and concern related to it should begin with the visually impaired infant, teachers of the visually impaired place emphasis on more formalized listening skills during the preschool years. These listening skills will ultimately lay part of the foundations for preacademic and later academic learning for the visually impaired child, and they are also important in unacademic, more functional areas. Preacademic skills are also addressed by the teacher of the visually impaired, who secures adaptive materials (including braille books, large-print materials, and Talking Books) and equipment (such as braillewriters, closed-circuit televisions [CCTVs], and specialized computers) in order to maximize the participation of visually impaired preschoolers in classrooms with sighted peers.

Teachers of visually impaired students address concept development, which needs to be formulated in a formal manner with young visually impaired children. They are also concerned with self-help skills (for example, eating, dressing, personal hygiene, personal organization, and toileting), which will not be acquired automatically by the child through observation. Socioemotional needs are addressed as the teacher supports the child in family and peer interactions while attempting to build social and play skills that facilitate the development of self-esteem. When necessary, teachers of the visually impaired may assist preschool staff and families with behavior management strategies that may be applicable to some young visually impaired children. For example, preschool staff may be confused about their role in dealing with the self-stimulating behaviors of some young blind children. The teacher of the visually impaired may have to suggest appropriate strategies to reduce such behaviors.

Aspects of communication that may need remediation, including receptive and expressive language, are important parts of the teacher's role because this specialist is very sensitive to the amount of nonverbal communication on which young visually impaired children miss out. Vision specialists also understand the need to provide instruction in nonverbal communication so that visually impaired children are able to make use of appropriate gestures that are integral components of communication. Vocational education is another mandated area the specialist should begin to address during the preschool period. As the visually impaired child grows older, the teacher of visually impaired students continues to work to promote optimum sensory development and purposeful functional usage of those sensory capabilities, including visual efficiency.

The O&M specialist is another vital team member in programs for young visually impaired children. He or she is particularly qualified in the following areas:

- Conducting home or school environmental assessments to suggest modifications to enhance motivation for movement or provide additional safety during independent movement,
- Completing specialized assessments, including functional vision assessments and assessments of O&M,
- Adapting assessment materials and procedures for other specialists, such as PTs, OTs, and adaptive physical educators,
- Interpreting medical and functional eye reports for related professionals and families,
- Providing in-service training for preschool staff and students,
- Securing adaptive materials and equipment related to O&M,
- Providing direct services to visually impaired children and their families in center- or home-based programs,
- Serving as a consultant to families and related professionals.

In providing direct service to young visually impaired children, the O&M specialist may address movement-related areas of development affected by vision loss. For visually impaired infants, particular emphasis may be placed on visual, auditory, tactile, olfactory, and kinesthetic development. The O&M specialist should be involved in designing immediate and surrounding environments that may motivate increased exploration and movement. O&M specialists may also assist families in developing caretaking practices that encourage young visually impaired children to become active participants in activities of daily living.

When working with visually impaired toddlers and preschoolers, the O&M specialist may focus on developing safe and efficient forms of independent movement for the child. Instruction in basic skills (such as sighted guide and protective techniques) for the blind child, the family, and associated friends and peers may begin during this period. It is also the role of the O&M specialist to introduce appropriate devices for use within the home, at school, in the community, or during O&M lessons. The long cane, the most prominent mobility device, may be specially ordered or individually modified in accordance with the size, weight, and strength of the individual preschool blind child.

The O&M specialist may also address areas of concept development that have a direct impact on the ability to travel independently. These areas may include body imagery, spatial relations, and environmental awareness. The foundations of map reading, map use, and personal-space organization may begin as a part of the O&M specialist's direct instruction. The specialist may also be involved in training young children for the use of low vision devices, especially such distance devices as monoculars and telescopes. It is the O&M specialist's role to develop and encourage the use of any existing vision that might improve the young child's independent functioning.

Many other professionals, including pediatric ophthalmologists, optometrists specializing in low vision, PTs, OTs, speech therapists, psychologists, adaptive physical educators, social workers, counselors, nurses, special educators, early childhood specialists, and teachers, may be involved with young visually impaired children and their families. The extent of that involvement is most likely to depend on the individual needs of the child and his or her family, the availability of services in the area, and the administrative structure and philosophies of the social or educational program that is providing services.

Many of the roles for teachers of visually impaired students, O&M specialists, and related professionals seem to overlap, or at least to closely shadow one another. This overlap may especially be in evidence when these professional's are working with visually impaired infants and their families. At this early stage in the child's life, all the professionals involved want to optimize the child's general development, which will ultimately have an impact on their specialty area. Professionals are jointly interested in supporting families and serving as resources to families who may need information or relevant contacts. It should not be surprising that many of their goals and objectives reflect this intent.

OVERLAP OF ROLES AND SERVICES

Professionals may often overlap in their direct service roles, and because assessment of young visually impaired children frequently is not a clearly defined area of responsibility, overlap in assessment services may frequently be seen. Although it is accepted that teachers of the visually impaired are responsible for assessing braille readiness skills, what about areas of concept development that may overlap with areas of concern for the O&M specialist? Which specialist should assess body imagery? It is clearly accepted that the O&M specialist is responsible for assessing independent travel skills,

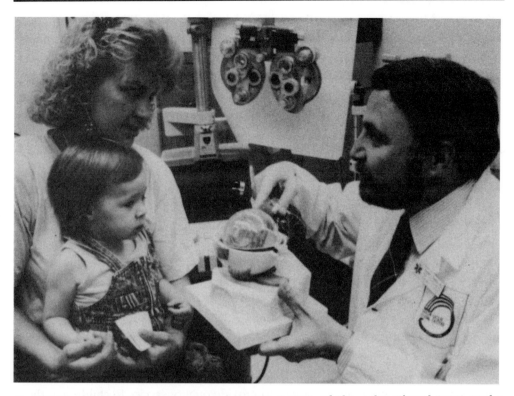

Pediatric ophthalmologists are an important part of the educational team and a source of valuable information for children's families.

but what about visual efficiency? And which specialist should assess functional vision? It is not always clear who is most appropriate to administer a given assessment or which is the most efficient way to complete a comprehensive assessment of the young visually impaired child.

Professionals in related fields, who may be most qualified to do assessments of speech and of fine and gross motor development, may be less familiar than are the vision specialist and O&M specialist with the impact of vision loss. When appropriate, these specialists should provide assistance (such as suggesting modifications for assessment items that require visual processing, helping to interpret responses of multiply impaired young children, and assisting in the administration of assessments to increase the quantity and quality of students' responses) to other professionals who are asked to assess the young visually impaired child. Suggestions for best positioning or seating, for optimum lighting and glare reduction, and for adaptation of assessment materials and procedures may help to obtain a more accurate picture of the visually impaired child's developmental potential. Assessments conducted cooperatively among vision specialists, O&M specialists, and other professionals may increase the efficiency and accuracy of the overall assessment of the child. The sharing of information at the assessment level improves the ability of families and professionals to interpret the assessment results. Increased understanding of results, in turn, better enables team members to make appropriate programming decisions for the visually impaired child and the family.

In regard to assessment as well as service delivery, the transdisciplinary approach inherently reduces the amount of overlap among professional responsibility common in work with visually impaired infants, toddlers, and preschoolers. Implementation of this approach can therefore be one way to reduce the overlap of professional roles. When considerations of what is most appropriate for visually impaired infants, toddlers, and preschoolers come into play, the transdisciplinary model limits the number of different professionals who work directly with the young child. Professionals from different disciplines provide information, training, and consultation to the staff members working directly with the child. This same kind of role release occurs during the assessment process, as professionals give input and make observations during assessment but the number of specialists who actually perform the hands-on assessment is limited. Additionally, the transdisciplinary model may limit the number of specialists with whom families must deal directly in the home, at school, or at agencies. For example, the teacher of visually impaired children may assume the primary service delivery role for a specific child. The OT or PT may share specific positioning techniques for the child with the teacher, while the O&M specialist may provide consultation on environmental considerations at home. The family would deal consistently with just one professional, but that one professional would have the benefit of shared expertise from two others. The transdisciplinary model appropriates professional resources in a way that reduces the redundancy of service delivery in early childhood and enhances the ability of professionals to provide quality service to children in their caseload.

For agencies and educational systems that do not employ the transdisciplinary model, effective organization and open communication among professionals can be helpful in minimizing role overlap. In general, one key to diminishing assessment and direct service overlap is organization. When professionals work together to preplan assessments, redundancy can be reduced or eliminated. If vision specialists and O&M specialists develop their caseloads in working cooperation, young visually impaired children can be assigned to individual specialists based on assessed needs rather than random selection. When programming decisions are made by professionals as a team, unnecessary direct service overlap can be eliminated before it is begun. Proper staff organization of staff resources should not only maximize the quality of service but should also minimize the confusion often experienced by young visually impaired children and their families.

In situations where professional responsibilities do overlap, cooperation and open communication are essential. Exploring service delivery options together may help professionals more clearly define their individual roles with the young visually impaired child. Through open discussions, they may find that not all vision specialists or O&M specialists are alike.

Although university training programs are similar in regard to many standards and competency areas, different universities may emphasize work with populations of different ages (adults, school-age or preschool children, or infants) in their training. Course offerings, such as electives in child development, early childhood special education, parent-professional collaboration, and the like, may be dependent on the expertise and interest of the university teaching staff or staff in associated departments, which may or may not be present on any given campus. Open discussions can help professionals to become more familiar with co-workers' backgrounds and training.

It is also important for professionals to explore previous teaching experiences with one another. These positive or negative experiences may have a genuine impact on the specialist's skills. Prior experiences may help to highlight individual teaching strengths and areas for support that are important to service delivery.

The personal components of enthusiasm and interest level are also important factors in determining which specialist would be better qualified to provide direct service in a particular area. Although many specialists may be well rounded in training and experience, it is not unusual to find people who have developed strong interests in working with specific populations, in teaching specific skills, or in assessing specific areas of development in young visually impaired children. These areas of interest often blossom into areas of professional expertise.

Service delivery models for visually impaired infants, toddlers, preschoolers, and their families may vary in philosophy, structure, professional training, and assessment and service delivery approaches. A wide array of program options enables families and professionals to explore various models in order to determine the program that will most closely meet the assessed needs of a particular visually impaired child.

ADVOCACY FOR YOUNG VISUALLY IMPAIRED CHILDREN

Like other children, young visually impaired children have difficulty advocating for themselves. Thus the role of advocate or active supporter falls mainly on others who believe in and are concerned with the development of the young child. Families and professionals in the field of visual impairment must be the key advocates for visually impaired infants and preschoolers. Parents and professionals working together as a team create the strongest advocacy force. It is often when things are not going well that the need for advocacy arises. Advocacy can be the force for change to improve services, communication, laws, policies, and rights. It is through advocacy in its many forms that positive changes occur that can significantly influence the lives of young visually impaired children.

Families are often thrown into advocacy without the tools to be successful. They are often expected to and forced to become advocates for their child upon recognition that the child has a visual impairment. The first time parents become advocates may be at the hospital or with medical personnel when they are told to make difficult decisions about their child's medical needs. These decisions may have to be made when they are emotionally distraught or in shock. They learn very quickly that in most cases, they are the ones ultimately required to make critical decisions on behalf of their child. They may feel intimidated by medical personnel and other "experts" who advise them on the best path. Without effective tools of advocacy, they may allow others to make decisions that may not always be in their child's best interest.

As the young visually impaired child grows older, parents may need to advocate for appropriate intervention services, related services such as PT, OT, or O&M program options, equipment and materials, and the like. Advocacy may occur in relation to the IFSP or IEP process, when goals and objectives are prioritized. Changes may occur at the local level in all these areas through effective advocacy. Parents should be made aware of their rights to due process so that they can have access to proper channels should there be unresolvable disagreements. Maintaining a nonadversarial attitude throughout any due process procedures and keeping the focus on the needs of the child help ensure ongoing team relationships between parents and professionals.

Some parents discover that advocacy within a local program does not bring about change, and they find themselves forced to advocate on a broader basis. Often the roadblocks to obtaining the necessary services for their child are outside local schools or agencies. These roadblocks may occur at the state or federal policy or legislative level. Advocating for changes in policy or law at the state or federal level can be started by one parent who feels a particular law or policy is harmful to his or her child, but most changes in the law come about through active support or advocacy on the part of many concerned individuals. There is usually therefore an initiator who recognizes that power exists in numbers. Joining together with other families of visually impaired children, and sometimes with families of children with other disabilities, creates a stronger voice to be heard by policymakers. Family members who become vocal advocates have made many significant changes in the law, including the passage of P.L. 94-142. Parents who believe their young visually impaired child should be taught by someone knowledgeable about the impact of vision loss on learning, for example, may advocate for changes in state teacher-certification laws that do not require disability-specific credentialing for teachers who work with visually impaired children.

Professionals in the field of visual impairment, especially those who work with families of young visually impaired children, must take on the role of advocate as one of their primary roles. Because of the low incidence of visually impaired children, few voices are speaking out who are knowledgeable about this population's unique needs. Strong voices are needed in working with medical and social service personnel, at the local school and agency level, and at the state and federal policymaking levels. Because of their unique expertise, specialized vision professionals are often the most qualified to facilitate needed changes. Professionals in the field of visual impairment no longer have the luxury of remaining apolitical. If they do not become active, vocal advocates for the children and families they serve, others less knowledgeable will make significant decisions that directly, and often negatively, affect the lives of visually impaired children.

The most powerful advocacy teams are those made up of both parents and professionals. A professional who is knowledgeable about the laws, the system, and appropriate educational services and strategies, paired with a parent who knows what is best for his or her child and who has the passion and commitment to communicate these beliefs, forms a voice that cannot easily be ignored. It is important in many situations that this team work together. It is also equally important that professionals assist parents in obtaining their own advocacy tools so that when the parents move on to other settings and advocacy arenas as their child gets older, they feel capable and competent to advocate on their own should they not have a professional teammate. Effective advocacy tools may be used throughout the years as a child develops. It is also important that parents and professionals begin giving the young visually impaired child his or her own advocacy tools and strategies as soon as possible so that the goal of self-advocacy can be realized. Ultimately, the child will have to learn how to advocate for changes on his or her own behalf.

There are a variety of arenas and ways in which one can be an advocate for young visually impaired children. These include:

- Supporting IFSP or IEP development and implementation,
- Ensuring that families know their due process rights,
- Ensuring the availability of appropriate specialized personnel at the local level,
- Ensuring the availability of an appropriate array of program options at the local level,
- Ensuring that appropriate medical and social services are available to families,
- Assisting with the recruitment of trainees for personnel preparation programs in the areas of visual impairment and O&M, with a focus on early childhood so that specialized personnel will be available,
- Joining professional or parent organizations,
- Staying informed about current issues and trends within the field by reading organizational newsletters, serving on boards, serving on legislative committees, going to conferences, and so on.
- Assisting advocacy groups and organizations financially or by volunteering to raise funds for them,
- Educating friends, family members, and co-workers about the needs of visually impaired children and about current problems, as they are the constituents of the decision makers,
- Meeting with state and federal legislators or their staff assistants to educate them about the needs of visually impaired children and about current problems (families and professionals need to remember that they know more about this area than any public official making decisions),
- Writing letters and making phone calls on relevant policies and bills at the state or federal level that may affect visually impaired children,
- Writing editorials for local newspapers informing the public about the needs of visually impaired children and current problems with service delivery, policies, laws, and so on,
- Participating as a member of interagency coordinating councils developed at local and state levels as a result of P.L. 99-457 (these councils often do not have representation by individuals knowledgeable about the unique needs of visually impaired infants and preschoolers),
- Joining or forming coalitions of consumers, parents, professionals, and agencies with common concerns about the rights and needs of young visually impaired children,

- Providing testimony at public hearings, hearings before legislative committees, and in similar situations on any issue affecting young visually impaired children.

In addition, basic guidelines and tools for effective advocacy include the following:

- Be assertive in communicating concerns (not passive or aggressive).
- Have a clear goal in mind when asking for change—what is it specifically that you want?
- Have a brief written statement of your concern, proposed change or solution, and rationale ready to give to any policymaker who may be unfamiliar with the issue.
- Go through proper channels first to see if a problem can be solved at a lower level instead of going straight to the top.
- Find out who is responsible for current policy so that time is not wasted with the wrong persons.
- Utilize personal contact with public officials, if appropriate, in order to get to see them.
- Use a public relations approach by inviting a public official to speak at a meeting or event and inviting the media for publicity.
- Use positive, polite communication skills when advocating—do not be intimidated, argumentative, or condescending.
- Advocate with no more than two or three people at a time, with at least one articulate spokesperson and the others for support.
- When writing letters or meeting with policymakers, always ask for a response to your request or their position on the issue.
- Be prepared by doing your homework before a meeting, but admit you do not know something if you do not, and offer to find out and get back to those present later.
- Negotiate, negotiate, negotiate! Realistic compromise without giving up your cause or principle is the key to successful advocacy.

It is important to realize that not all individuals have the same energy or time available for advocacy. Some families may choose not to participate in advocacy activities, either because their focus and energy are directed toward more basic human needs or because they simply prefer not to become involved. This is their right. Families and professionals alike may vary in their abilities to contribute to important causes at different times in their lives. If all individuals concerned about young visually impaired children are willing to do what they can, from testifying at a hearing to folding fliers at home for a mailing, the process of advocacy will be vital and effective. Everyone doing something is what makes the difference in effecting positive changes.

Realizing that most advocacy efforts do not create immediate changes helps one focus more realistically on the process of advocacy. Advocacy begins with the planting of seeds that over time, and with nourishment, lead to desired results. In the legislative arena, for example, the process often begins with focusing on the language of legislative intent, followed by mandating a law, followed by a budget bill that provides the necessary funding to carry out the original intent. Patience and persistence are essential to successful advocacy.

It is often momentary crises that fuel the fires of advocacy. It is, however, important to look ahead and to be farsighted in determining when one should be proactive for the future. Families and professionals advocating for the needs of infants and preschoolers should also be ensuring that programs, services, and safeguards for rights will be in place as these children enter future educational and rehabilitative arenas. Considering the evolutionary process of system change, it is important that a long-term perspective be taken as one clears the pathway for the young visually impaired children of today and ensures that appropriate services will be available for the children of the future.

References

Ayres, A. J. (1979). *Sensory integration and the child.* Los Angeles: Western Psychological Services.

Banos, B. (1971). *The developmental therapist.* Thorofare, NJ: Charles B. Slack.

Bobath, K. (1974). *The motor deficit in patients with cerebral palsy.* London: Lavenham Press.

Brown, C., & Bour, B. (1986). Movement analysis and curriculum for visually impaired preschoolers. In *A Resource Manual for the Development and Evaluation of Special Programs for Exceptional Students: Vol. V-K.* Tallahassee, FL: Florida Bureau of Education for Exceptional Students, Department of Education.

Brown, L., Nietupski, J., & Hamre-Nietupski, S. (1976). The criterion of ultimate functioning and public school services for severely handicapped children. In M. A. Thomas (Ed.), *Hey, Don't Forget about Me!* Reston, VA: Council for Exceptional Children.

Clarke, K. (1988). Barriers or enablers? Mobility devices for visually impaired multihandicapped infants and preschoolers. *Education of the Visually Handicapped, 20,* 115-132.

Coley, I. L. (1978). *Pediatric assessment of self-care activities.* St. Louis, MO: C.V. Mosby.

Combs, G. W. (1980). Defensive and supportive communication. In J. W. Pfeiffer & J. E. Jones (Eds.), *Structured Experience Kit.* San Diego, CA: University Associates.

Corn, A. (1983). Visual function: A theoretical model for individuals with low vision. *Journal of Visual Impairment & Blindness, 77(8),* 373-377.

Cratty, B. (1964). *Movement behavior and motor learning.* Philadelphia: Lea & Febinger.

Cratty, B. (1971). *Movement and spatial awareness in blind children and youth.* Springfield, IL: Charles C Thomas.

Cratty, B.J., & Sams, T.A. (1968). *The body-image of blind children.* New York: American Foundation for the Blind.

Cross, D. P. (1981). Physical disabilities. In A. E. Blackhurst & W.H. Berdine (Eds.), *An Introduction to Special Education.* Boston: Little, Brown.

Curry, S. A., & Hatlen, P. H. (1988). Meeting the unique educational needs of visually impaired pupils through appropriate placement. *Journal of Visual Impairment & Blindness, 82(10),* 417-424.

Cutsforth, T. D. (1951). *The blind in school and society.* New York: American Foundation for the Blind.

Eagar, G. R. (1986). Chicano and Hispanic families. In *Reaching Out: Proceedings from a Special Education Symposium on Cultural Differences and Parent Programs* (pp. 49-55). Eugene, OR: Western Regional Resource Center.

Falvey, M. A. (1986). *Community-based curriculum: Instructional strategies for students with severe handicaps.* Baltimore, MD: Paul H. Brookes.

Ferrell, K. A. (1985). *Reach out and teach: Meeting the training needs of parents of visually and multiply handicapped young children.* New York: American Foundation for the Blind.

Fraiberg, S. (1970). Smiling and stranger reaction in blind infants. In J. Hellmath (Ed.), *Exceptional Infant.* New York: Brunner-Mazel.

Fraiberg, S. (1977). *Insights from the blind: Comparative studies of blind and sighted infants.* New York: Basic Books.

Gesell, A. (1949). *Vision, its development in infant and child*. New York: Harper & Row.

Gesell, A., & Armatruda, C. (1974). *Developmental diagnosis: The evaluation and management of normal and abnormal neuropsychologic development in infancy and early childhood*. New York: Harper & Row.

Gleason, D. (1984). Auditory assessment of visually impaired preschoolers: A team effort. *Education of the Visually Handicapped, 16(3)*, 106.

Gold, M. W. (1980). *"Try another way" training manual*. Champaign, IL: Research Press.

Hatlen, P. H. (February 1990). Testimony presented to the Least Restrictive Environment Study Team of the Los Angeles Unified School District for the Joint Action Committee of Organizations Of and Serving the Visually Handicapped.

Hatlen, P. H., & Curry, S. A. (1987). In support of specialized programs for visually impaired children: The impact of vision loss on learning. *Journal of Visual Impairment & Blindness, 81(1)*, 7-13.

Hazekamp, J., & Huebner, K. M. (1989). *Program planning and evaluation for blind and visually impaired students: National guidelines for educational excellence*. New York: American Foundation for the Blind.

Heininger, M., & Randolph, S. (1981). *Neurophysiological concepts in human behavior: The tree of learning*. St. Louis, MO: C.V. Mosby.

Hill, E. W. (1981). *The Hill performance test of selected positional concepts*. Chicago: Stoelting.

Hill, E. W. (1988). *Preschool orientation and mobility project for visually impaired children: Final Report*. (Project No. 024AH 40132). Nashville, TN: Vanderbilt University, Peabody College. (ERIC Document Service No. ED 292 259).

Hill, E. W., Dodson-Burk, B., & Smith, B. (1989). Orientation and mobility for infants who are visually impaired. *RE:View, 21(2)*, 47-59.

Hill, E.W., & Ponder, P. (1976). *Orientation and mobility techniques: A guide for the practitioner*. New York: American Foundation for the Blind.

Hill, E. W., Rosen, S., Correa, V., & Langley, M. (1984). Preschool orientation and mobility: An expanded definition. *Education of the Visually Handicapped, 16*, 58-72.

Hutchinson, D. A. (1974). A model for transdisciplinary staff development. In *A Nationally Organized Collaborative Program for the Provision of Comprehensive Services to Atypical Infants and Their Families* (Technical Report No. 8). New York: United Cerebral Palsy Association.

Jan, J. E., Robinson, G. C., Scott, E., & Kinnis, C. (1975). Hypotonia in the blind child. *Developmental Medicine & Child Neurology, 17*, 25-40.

Kastein, S., Spaulding, I., & Scharf, B. (1980). *Raising the young blind child: A guide for parents and educators*. New York: Human Sciences Press.

Keith, C. G., & Kitchens, W. H. (1983). Ocular morbidity in infants of very low birth weight. *British Journal of Ophthalmology, 67(5)*, 302-305.

Langley, M.B. (1980). *Functional vision inventory for the multiple and severely handicapped*. Chicago: Stoelting.

Langley, M. B. (1980). *Peabody model vision project*. Chicago: Stoelting.

Lighthouse cards. (1980). New York: New York Association for the Blind.

Lyon, S., & Lyon, G. (1980). Team functioning and staff development: A role release approach to providing integrated educational services for severely handicapped students. *Journal of the Association for the Severely Handicapped, 5(3)*, 250-263.

Morse, A. R., & Trief, E. (1985). Diagnosis and evaluation of visual dysfunction in premature infants with low birth weight. *Journal of Visual Impairment & Blindness, 79(6)*, 248-251.

Moskowitz, B. (1978). The development of language. *Scientific American*, 82-96.

Mullings-Franco, P. (1987). *The urban black family*. Paper presented at Reaching Out to Families in a Multicultural Society Conference, Santa Fe, NM.

Nirje, B. (1969). The normalization principle and its management implications. In R. Kugel & W. Wolfensberger (Eds.), *Changing Patterns in Residential Services for the Mentally Retarded* (pp. 51-57). Washington, DC: U.S. Government Printing Office.

Parsons, S. (1986). Function of play in low vision children (Part 1): A review of the research and literature. *Journal of Visual Impairment & Blindness, 80(3),* 627-630.

Parsons visual acuity test. (1979). South Bend, IN: Bernell Corporation.

Perske, R., & Smith, J. (1977). *Interdisciplinary and transdisciplinary teamwork.* Seattle, WA: AAE-SPH Review.

Pogrund, R. L., & Rosen, S. J. (1989). The preschool blind child *can* be a cane user. *Journal of Visual Impairment & Blindness, 83,* 431-439.

Salcedo, P. (1986). Coping with the coping process. *Bridges, 3,* 1-2.

Schinke, S. P., Gilchrist, L. D., & Small, R. W. (1979). Preventing unwanted adolescent pregnancy: A cognitive-behavioral approach. *American Journal of Orthopsychiatry, 49(1),* 81-88.

Tager-Flushberg, H. (1985). Putting words together: Morphology and syntax in the preschool years. In J. B. Gleason (Ed.), *The Development of Language.* Columbus, OH: Charles E. Merrill.

Thorp, E., & Brown, C. (1987). *The family experience: A module of Project Year One—A comprehensive training package for infant service providers.* Washington, DC: George Washington University School of Education and Human Development, Department of Special Education, Infant Education Program.

Trief, E., Duckman, R., Morse, A. R., & Silberman, R. K. (1989). Retinopathy of prematurity. *Journal of Visual Impairment & Blindness, 83(10),* 500-504.

Tyler, N., & Chandler, L. (1978). The developmental therapists: Occupational therapists and physical therapists. In K. E. Allen et al. (Eds.), *Early Intervention: A Team Approach.* Baltimore, MD: University Park Press.

Uslan, M. (1983). Provision of orientation and mobility services in 1990. *Journal of Visual Impairment & Blindness, 77(5),* 213-215.

Vision screening project. (1980). Parsons, KS: University of Kansas Bureau of Child Research.

Warren, D. H. (1984). *Blindness and early childhood development* (2nd ed., rev.). New York: American Foundation for the Blind.

Yano, C. (1986). Asian families. In *Reaching Out: Proceedings from a Special Education Symposium on Cultural Differences and Parent Programs* (pp. 39-47). Eugene, OR: Western Regional Resource Center.

Resources

Books

Alonso, L., Moor, P. M., Raynor, S., von Hippel, C., & Baer, S. *Mainstreaming preschoolers: Children with visual handicaps*. (DHEW publication #OHDS 78-31112). Washington, DC: Superintendent of Documents, U.S. Government Printing Office.

Bailey, D. B., & Woolery, M. (1989). *Assessing infants and preschoolers with handicaps*. Columbus, OH: Merrill Publishing.

Bailey, I. L., & Hall, A. (1990). *Visual impairment: An overview*. New York: American Foundation for the Blind.

Barraga, N. (1970). *Teacher's guide for development of visual learning abilities and utilization of low vision*. Louisville, KY: American Printing House for the Blind.

Bernstein, J. (1988). *Loving Rachel: A parent's journey from grief*. Boston: Little, Brown.

Bower, T. G. R. (1982). *Development in infancy* (2nd ed.). San Francisco: W.H. Freeman.

Bradley-Johnson, S. (1986). *Psychoeducational assessment of visually impaired and blind students*. Austin, TX: Pro-Ed.

Brennan, M. (1982). *Show me how: A manual for parents of preschool visually impaired and blind children*. New York: American Foundation for the Blind.

Bureau of Education for Exceptional Students, State of Florida (1983). *Project IVEY: Increasing visual efficiency: Vol. V-E*. Tallahassee, FL: Florida Department of Education.

Bureau of Education for Exceptional Students, State of Florida (1987). *Movement analysis and curriculum for visually impaired preschoolers: Vol. V-K*. Tallahassee, FL: Florida Department of Education.

Collins, M. S. (1982). *Parental reactions to a visually handicapped child: A mourning process*. Unpublished doctoral dissertation, University of Texas.

Cratty, B. J. (1970). *Perceptual motor development in infants and children*. New York: Macmillan.

Cratty, B. J., & Sams, T. A. (1968). *The body-image of blind children*. New York: American Foundation for the Blind.

Dodson-Burk, B., & Hill, E. W. (1989). *An orientation and mobility primer for families and young children*. New York: American Foundation for the Blind.

Drouillard, R., & Raynor, S. (1977). *Move it*. Lanham, MD: American Alliance Publications.

Ensher, G. L., & Clark, D. A. (1986). *Newborns at risk: Medical care and psychoeducational intervention*. Rockville, MD: Aspen Publishers.

Ferrell, K. A. (1985). *Reach out and teach: Meeting the training needs of parents of visually and multiply handicapped young children*. New York: American Foundation for the Blind.

Fetherstone, H. (1980). *A difference in the family*. New York: Penguin Books.

Finnie, N. R. (1975). *Handling the young cerebral palsied child at home* (2nd ed.). New York: E.P. Dutton.

Fraiberg, S. (1977). *Insights from the blind: Comparative studies of blind and sighted infants*. New York: Basic Books.

Freeman, P. (1975). *Understanding the deaf-blind child*. London: Heinemann Health Books.

Galante, J. S. (1981). *Workbook for parents & teachers: Teaching the visually impaired preschool child 2-5 years old*. Buffalo, NY: Buffalo Public Schools.

Goldberg, S. (1982). *Ophthalmology made ridiculously simple.* Miami, FL: Medical Master.

Halliday, C. (1971). *The visually impaired child: Growth, learning, developmental infancy to school age.* Louisville, KY: American Printing House for the Blind.

Harrell, L., & Akeson, N. (1987). *Preschool vision stimulation: It's more than a flashlight!* New York: American Foundation for the Blind.

Hazekamp, J., & Huebner, K. M. (1989). *Program planning and evaluation for blind and visually impaired students: National guidelines for educational excellence.* New York: American Foundation for the Blind.

Helmut, P. (1978). *Games and toys for blind children in preschool age.* Paris: World Council for the Welfare of the Blind.

Illinois State Board of Education (1972). *Preschool learning activities for the visually impaired: A guide for parents.* Arlington Heights, VA: ERIC Document Reproduction Service.

Isenberg, S. J. (1989). *The eye in infancy.* Chicago: Year Book Medical Publishers.

Jose, R. T. (1983). *Understanding low vision.* New York: American Foundation for the Blind.

Kastein, S., Spaulding, I., & Scharf, B. (1980). *Raising the young blind child: A guide for parents and educators.* New York: Human Sciences Press.

Lowenfeld, B. (1971). *Our blind children* (3rd ed.). Springfield, IL: Charles C Thomas.

Lydon, W. T., & McGraw, M. L. (1973). *Concept development for visually handicapped children.* New York: American Foundation for the Blind.

McClannahan, C. (1989). *Feeding and caring for infants & children with special needs.* Rockville, MD: American Occupational Therapy Association.

Nousanen, D., & Robinson, L. W. (1980). *Take charge! A guide to resources for parents of the visually impaired.* Beloit, WI: National Association for Parents of the Visually Impaired.

Raynor, S., & Drouillard, R. (1975). *Get a wiggle on: A guide for helping visually impaired children grow.* Lanham, MD: American Alliance Publications.

Rogow, S. M. (1988). *Helping the visually impaired child with developmental problems.* New York: Teachers College Press.

Savage, S. (1973). *Instructional programming for the severely handicapped: The individualized critical skills model (ICSM).* Sacramento, CA: State Department of Education.

Scholl, G. T. (Ed.). (1986). *Foundations of education for blind and visually handicapped children and youth.* New York: American Foundation for the Blind.

Scott, E. P., Jon, J. E., & Freeman, R. D. (1985). *Can't your child see?* Austin, TX: Pro-Ed.

Silverman, W. A., & Flynn, J. T. (1985). *Retinopathy of prematurity.* Boston: Blackwell Scientific Publications.

Smith, A. J., & Cote, K. S. (1982). *Look at me: A resource manual for the development of residual vision in multiply impaired children.* Philadelphia, PA: Pennsylvania College of Optometry Press.

Swallow, R., & Huebner, K. M. (1987). *How to thrive, not just survive.* New York: American Foundation for the Blind.

Tingey, C. (1989). *Implementing early intervention.* Baltimore, MD: Paul H. Brookes Publishing.

Tuttle, D. W. (1984). *Self esteem and adjusting with blindness.* Springfield, IL: Charles C Thomas.

Vaughan, D., Asbury, T., & Tabbara, K. F. (1989). *General ophthalmology* (12th ed.). East Norwalk, CT: Appleton and Lange.

Warren, D. H. (1984). *Blindness and early childhood development* (2nd ed., rev.). New York: American Foundation for the Blind.

Watson, M. J., & Nicholas, J. L. (1973). *A practical guide to the training of low functioning deaf-blind.* Hartford, CT: Connecticut Institute for the Blind.

Booklets and Pamphlets

Baby care basics. (1988). Skillman, NJ: Johnson & Johnson Baby Care Products Company.

Ballard, J., Ramirez, B., & Zantal-Weiner, K. (1989). *Public Law 94-142, Section 504, and Public Law 99-457: Understanding what they are and are not.* Reston, VA: Council for Exceptional Children.

Ferrell, K. A. (1984). *Parenting preschoolers: Suggestions for raising young blind and visually impaired children.* New York: American Foundation for the Blind.

Getting to know your newborn. (1987). Skillman, NJ: Johnson & Johnson Baby Care Products Company.

Harrell, L. (1984). *Touch the baby.* New York: American Foundation for the Blind.

Hedgecock, H., Hudson, E., Del Castillo, E., Stotland, J., & Sael, E. *Legislative handbook for parents.* Beloit, WI: National Association for Parents of the Visually Impaired.

How your baby grows. (1979). Skillman, NJ: Johnson & Johnson Baby Care Products Company.

Hug, D., Chernus-Mansfield, N., & Hayashi, P. *Move with me: A parent's guide to movement development for visually impaired babies.* Los Angeles: Blind Childrens Center.

Kekelis, L. (1984). *Talk to me: A language guide for parents of blind children.* Los Angeles: Blind Childrens Center.

Kekelis, L. (1985). *Talk to me II: Common concerns.* Los Angeles: Blind Childrens Center.

Meyers, L., & Lansky, P. (1991). *Dancing cheek to cheek: Nurturing beginning social, play, and language interactions.* Los Angeles: Blind Childrens Center.

Mulholland, M. E., & Wurster, M. V. (Eds.) (1983). *Help me become everything I can be: Proceedings of North American Conference on Visually Handicapped Infants and Preschool Children.* New York: American Foundation for the Blind.

Murray, V. (undated). *Hints for parents of preschool visually handicapped children.* San Francisco, CA: Variety Club Blind Babies Foundation.

Parents, team up with your school: A handbook to help your special child. (1980). Carson, CA: Harbor Regional Center for Developmentally Disabled Citizens, Inc.

Recchia, S. (1985). *Heart to heart: Parents of blind and partially sighted children talk about their feelings.* Los Angeles: Blind Childrens Center.

Recchia, S. (undated). *Learning to play: Common concerns for the visually impaired preschool child.* Los Angeles: Blind Childrens Center.

Schuch, J. (1980). *Get ready, get set, go!* Lansing, MI: International Institute for Visually Impaired.

Some children are more special than others ... A guide to Mattel Toys for parents of the visually handicapped child. (1980-81). Hawthorne, CA: Mattel, Inc.

Assessments

Anthony, T. *Early intervention: Orientation and mobility checklist.* 2211-B Arca Drive, Anchorage, AK 99508: Special Education Service Agency.

Assessment of auditory functioning of D-B/MH children. (1978). Dallas, TX: South Central Regional Center for Services to D-B Children.

Battelle developmental inventory. P.O. Box 400, Allen, TX 75002: DLM/Teaching Resources.

Bayley, N. (1969). *Bayley scales of infant development.* San Antonio, TX: The Psychological Corporation.

Brigance diagnostic inventory of early development. (1978). 5 Esquire Road, North Billerica, MA 01862-2589: Curriculum Associates.

Callier-Azusa Scale. (1978). 1966 Inwood Road, Dallas, TX, 75235: University of Texas at Dallas, Callier Center for Communication Disorders.

Carolina assessment for handicapped infants. (1986). P.O. Box 10624, Baltimore, MD 21285-0624: Paul H. Brookes Publishers.

Curriculum guide for deaf-blind students—Component III orientation and mobility. Philadelphia, PA: School District of Philadelphia, PA Regional Center for Deaf-Blind Children.

Davies, J. (1989). *Assessing infants who are visually impaired or deaf-blind for functional vision and orientation and mobility.* San Diego, CA: San Diego City Schools.

Dodson-Burk, B., & Hill, E. W. (1989). *Preschool orientation and mobility screening*. Alexandria, VA: Division IX of the Association for Education and Rehabilitation of the Blind and Visually Impaired.

Foundation for the Junior Blind Infant-Family Program: Curriculum outline and assessment checklist. (1984). Los Angeles: Foundation for the Junior Blind.

Hawaii early learning profile (H.E.L.P.). (1979). P.O. Box 11132, Palo Alto, CA 94306: VORT Corporation.

Hill, E. W. (1981). *The Hill performance test of selected positional concepts*. Chicago: Stoelting.

Langley, M. B. (1980). *Functional vision inventory for the multiply and severely handicapped*. Chicago: Stoelting.

Maxfield, K. E., & Buchholz, S. (1957). *A social maturity scale for blind preschool children. A guide to its use*. New York: American Foundation for the Blind.

Reynell-Zenkin scales: Developmental scales for young visually handicapped children. Chicago, IL: Stoelting.

Other Resources

Brown, D., Simmons, V., & Methvin, J. (1979). *Oregon project for visually impaired and blind preschoolers* [Assessment & Curriculum]. Medford, OR: Jackson County Education Service District.

Chen, D., Friedman, C. T., & Calvello, G. (1988). *Parents and visually impaired infants (PAVII)* [Guidelines & Materials]. Louisville, KY: American Printing House for the Blind.

Croft, N. B., & Robinson, L. W. (1984). *Growing up: A developmental curriculum* [Curriculum]. Beloit, WI: National Association for Parents of the Visually Impaired.

Davis, J. A., & Langley, M. B. (1980). *Peabody model vision project* [Curriculum]. Chicago: Stoelting.

Hill, E. W. (1987). *Preschool orientation and mobility project for visually impaired children: Final report, Grant No. G008401385* [Curriculum]. Washington, DC: HCEEP. (ERIC Document No. 292 259).

MacConnachie, J. (Producer). (1988). *Raising a little cane: Trends in teaching cane travel to preschoolers*. [Video]. Rimrock West—Box 29, Bend, OR 97701.

Moore, S. (Producer). (1985). *Beginnings: A practical guide for parents and teachers of visually impaired babies* [Booklet and Video]. Louisville, KY: American Printing House for the Blind.

Moses, K. (1974). *The mourning theory and family dynamics: A presentation for the parents and families of impaired children* [Video]. Peoria, IL: Regional Resource Center VII.

Project year one: A comprehensive training package for infant service providers: The family experience, the neonatal experience, and the community experience [Resource Manuals]. (1988). Washington, DC: George Washington University, School of Education and Human Development, Department of Special Education, Infant Education Program.

Your child's information journal [Organizational Packet]. Beloit, WI: National Association for Parents of the Visually Impaired.

Journals and Newsletters

Awareness
National Association for Parents of the Visually Impaired
2180 Linway Drive
Beloit, WI 53511

The Exceptional Parent
296 Boylston Street, Third Floor
Boston, MA 02116

Future Reflections
Box 552
Jefferson City, MO 65102

Journal of Visual Impairment & Blindness
Department of Publications and Information Services
American Foundation for the Blind
15 West 16th Street
New York, NY 10011

The National Newspatch: Quarterly Newsletter for Educators of Visually Impaired Preschoolers
Oregon School for the Blind
700 Church Street, S.E.
Salem, OR 97310

RE:view
Heldref Publications
1319 18th Street, N. W.
Washington, DC 20036-1802

Sibling Information Network
Department of Educational Psychology
Box U-64
The University of Connecticut
Storrs, CT 06268

The Special Edge: Resources in Special Education
California State University, Sacramento
650 Howe Avenue, Suite 300
Sacramento, CA 95825

The VIP Newsletter IIVI, 0-7 Inc.
1975 Rutgers
East Lansing, MI 48823

Organizations and Agencies

The items in this section are a selection of organizations on the national, state, and local levels which provide information, assistance, and referrals; operate toll-free hotlines; and publish materials that are valuable sources of information for parents of infants and preschool children who are blind or visually impaired and the professionals who work with them. A complete listing of agencies and organizations serving blind and visually impaired persons is included in the *Directory of Services for Blind and Visually Impaired Persons in the United States*, 23rd Edition, published by the American Foundation for the Blind.

American Association of the Deaf-Blind
814 Thayer Avenue
Silver Spring, MD 20910
(301) 588-6545

The American Association of the Deaf-Blind is a consumer organization of deaf-blind persons. It is involved in advocacy activities, conducts service programs, acts as a referral service, maintains a library of materials on deaf-blindness, and holds a convention annually for deaf-blind persons and their families.

American Council of the Blind—Parents
c/o American Council of the Blind
1155 15th Street, N.W.
Suite 720
Washington, DC 20005
(202) 467-5081

The American Council of the Blind—Parents is a special interest affiliate of the American Council of the Blind (ACB). It promotes the sharing of resources and information and produces an informative newsletter for parents of blind or visually impaired children. ACB is a consumer organization that provides referrals; scholarships; leadership and legislative training; consumer advocacy support; assistance in technological research; consultative and advisory services to individuals, organizations, and agencies; and program development assistance.

American Foundation for the Blind
11 Penn Plaza
New York, NY 10001
(212) 502-7600; (800) 232-5463 (Hotline)

The American Foundation for the Blind (AFB) provides direct and technical assistance services to blind and visually impaired persons and their families, professionals in specialized agencies for blind persons, community agencies, organizations, schools, and corporations. AFB provides legislative consultation; operates an Information Center encompassing the M.C. Migel Memorial Library, a special reference library on blindness; produces videos and publishes books, monographs, and periodicals in print, braille, and recorded formats; manufactures Talking Books; and informs the public about the latest technology available for blind and visually impaired persons. AFB also operates a toll-free information hotline. Its headquarters office addresses national issues and serves the states of Connecticut, Delaware, Maine, Massachusetts, New Hampshire, New Jersey, New York, Pennsylvania, Rhode Island, and Vermont. The following field offices are maintained across the United States:

AFB East
1615 M Street, N.W.
Suite 250
Washington, DC 20036
(202) 457-1487

Serves District of Columbia, Maryland, and Virginia.

AFB Midwest
401 N. Michigan Avenue
Suite 308
Chicago, IL 60611
(312) 245-9961

Serves Illinois, Indiana, Iowa, Kentucky, Michigan, Minnesota, Missouri, North Dakota, Ohio, South Dakota, Tennessee, West Virginia, and Wisconsin.

AFB Southeast
100 Peachtree Street
Suite 620
Atlanta, GA 30303
(404) 525-2303

Serves Georgia, Puerto Rico, and the Virgin Islands.

AFB Southwest
260 Treadway Plaza
Exchange Park
Dallas, TX 75235
(214) 352-7222

Serves Alabama, Arkansas, Colorado, Florida, Kansas, Louisiana, Mississippi, Montana, Nebraska, New Mexico, Oklahoma, Texas, and Wyoming.

AFB West
111 Pine Street
Suite 725
San Francisco, CA 94111
(415) 392-4845

Serves Alaska, Arizona, California, Guam, Hawaii, Idaho, Nevada, Oregon, Utah, and Washington.

American Printing House for the Blind
1839 Frankfort Avenue
Louisville, KY 40206
(502) 895-2405

The American Printing House for the Blind (APH) is a national organization that publishes books in braille, large-print, and audiotape formats; manufactures educational aids for blind and visually impaired persons; modifies and develops computer-access equipment and software; maintains an educational research and development program concerned with educational methods and educational aids; and provides a reference-catalog service for volunteer-produced textbooks in all media for visually impaired students and for information about other sources of related materials.

Association for Education and Rehabilitation of the Blind and Visually Impaired
206 North Washington Street
Suite 320
Alexandria, VA 22314
(703) 548-1884

The Association for Education and Rehabilitation of the Blind and Visually Impaired (AER) is a professional membership organization that promotes all phases of education and work for blind and visually impaired persons of all ages. AER organizes conferences and workshops, conducts certification programs for professionals working with people who are blind, maintains job-exchange services and a speakers' bureau, holds continuing-education seminars, and is involved in legislative and advocacy projects. AER also publishes RE:view—*a quarterly journal for professionals working in the field of blindness—and disseminates brochures and videotapes.*

The Association for Persons with Severe Handicaps
11201 Greenwood Avenue, North
Seattle, WA 98133
(206) 361-8870

The Association for Persons with Severe Handicaps (TASH) advocates for services for persons with severe disabilities. It also disseminates information and publishes a newsletter and a journal.

Blind Children's Fund
230 Central Street
Auburndale, MA 02166
(617) 332-4014

The Blind Children's Fund is an organization of parents and teachers that promotes activities and programs that benefit the growth, development, and education of visually impaired children. It also publishes pamphlets and books and holds symposia.

Canadian National Institute for the Blind
1931 Bayview Avenue
Toronto, Ontario M4G 4C8
Canada
(416) 480-7580

The Canadian National Institute for the Blind (CNIB) fosters the integration of blind and visually impaired persons into the mainstream of Canadian life and promotes programs for the prevention of blindness.

Council for Exceptional Children
1920 Association Drive
Reston, VA 22091
(703) 620-3660

The Council for Exceptional Children (CEC) advocates for the rights of exceptional individuals to achieve educational opportunities, career development, and equal employment access. CEC publishes periodicals and other materials on teaching disabled children. The Division for the Visually Handicapped is a professional organization of teachers, school administrators, and others who work with visually impaired children.

National Information Center for Handicapped Children and Youth
P.O. Box 1492
Washington, DC 20013
(703) 893-6061 or 800-999-5599; (703) 893-8614 (TDD)

The National Information Center for Handicapped Children and Youth is a free information service focusing on the needs of children and youth with disabilities. Its services include personal responses to specific questions, referrals, information packets, recruitment materials for careers in special education, publications, and technical assistance to groups of parents and professionals.

Hadley School for the Blind
700 Elm Street
Winnetka, Illinois 60093
(312) 446-8111; (800) 323-4238

The Hadley School for the Blind is an accredited home-study school. Its Parent/Child program offers parents of visually impaired children free course materials on assessing a child's abilities, developing an infant's sensory skills, and using sensory aids in teaching a child. It also provides a series of free booklets and periodicals and distributes the parents' handbook, Reach Out and Teach: Meeting the Training Needs of Parents of Visually and Multiply Handicapped Young Children.

Helen Keller National Center for Deaf-Blind Youths and Adults
111 Middle Neck Road
Sands Point, NY 11050
(516) 944-8900 (voice and TDD)

The Helen Keller National Center for Deaf-Blind Youths and Adults provides services and technical assistance to deaf-blind individuals and their families and maintains a network of regional and affiliate agencies.

National Association for Parents of the Visually Impaired
P.O. Box 317
Watertown, MA 02272-0317
(617) 972-7441; (800) 562-6265

The National Association for Parents of the Visually Impaired (NAPVI) provides support to parents and families of visually impaired children; operates a national clearinghouse for information, education, and referral; promotes public understanding of the needs and rights of visually impaired children; and supports state and local parents' groups and workshops that educate and train parents about available services and their children's rights.

National Association for Visually Handicapped
22 West 21st Street
New York, NY 10010
(212) 889-3141

The National Association for Visually Handicapped (NAVH) produces and distributes large-print reading materials; offers counseling to persons with low vision, their families, and the professionals who work with them; acts as an information clearinghouse and referral center; sells low vision devices; and publishes In Focus *(for children) and* Seeing Clearly *(for adults).*

National Center for Education in Maternal and Child Health
38th and R Streets, N.W.
Washington, DC 20057
(202) 625-8400

The National Center for Education in Maternal and Child Health provides information services to parents and professionals on maternal and child health. It operates a resource center containing books, journals, articles, teaching manuals, brochures, fact sheets, and audiovisual materials and annually publishes Reaching Out: A Directory of Organizations Related to Maternal Health.

National Coalition for Deaf-Blindness
c/o Perkins School for the Blind
175 North Beacon Street
Watertown, MA 02172
(617) 924-3434

The National Coalition for Deaf-Blindness advocates on behalf of deaf-blind persons and provides information to consumers and professionals.

National Council of State Agencies for the Blind
206 N. Washington Street, Suite 320
Alexandria, VA 22314
(703) 548-1885

The National Council of State Agencies for the Blind promotes communication among agencies serving persons who are severely visually impaired.

National Early Childhood Technical Assistance System
CB #8040
500 NCNB Plaza
Chapel Hill, NC 27599
(919) 962-2001

The National Early Childhood Technical Assistance System provides technical assistance on the implementation of P.L. 99-457.

National Federation of the Blind—Parents
1800 Johnson Street
Baltimore, MD 21230
(301) 659-9314

The National Federation of the Blind (NFB) is a national consumer organization with affiliates in all states. It monitors legislation affecting blind people, assists in promoting needed services, works to improve social and economic conditions of blind persons, provides evaluation of present programs and assistance in establishing new ones, grants scholarships to blind persons, and conducts a public education program.

National Library Service for the Blind and Physically Handicapped
Library of Congress
1291 Taylor Street, N.W.
Washington, DC 20542
(202) 707-5100; (800) 424-8567

The National Library Service (NLS) for the Blind and Physically Handicapped conducts a national program to distribute free reading materials in braille and on recorded disks and cassettes to visually impaired and physically disabled persons who cannot utilize ordinary printed materials.

National Organization for Albinism and Hypopigmentation
1500 Locust Street
Suite 1816
Philadelphia, PA 19102
(215) 454-2322

The National Organization for Albinism and Hypopigmentation (NOAH) publishes brochures and books to educate the public about albinism and hypopigmentation, encourages research on prevention and treatment of the diseases, holds conferences, maintains a speakers' bureau, and provides support to persons with albinism or hypopigmentation and their families.

Office of Disease Prevention and Health Promotion
National Health Information Center
P.O. Box 1133
Washington, DC 20013-1133
(301) 336-4797; (800) 336-4797

The Office of Disease Prevention and Health Promotion refers medical professionals and the public to appropriate health organizations, provides health-related information, and maintains a library and an internal database.

Office of Special Education Programs
Preschool Grants Office
400 Maryland Avenue, S.W.
Washington, DC 20202
(202) 732-1097

The Office of Special Education Programs provides general information on P.L. 99-457 and information about how to contact the individual state government bodies administering it.

RP Foundation Fighting Blindness
(National Retinitis Pigmentosa Foundation)
1401 Mt. Royal Avenue
Baltimore, MD 21217
(301) 225-9400

The RP Foundation Fighting Blindness conducts public education programs, supports research related to the prevention and treatment of retinitis pigmentosa, maintains a network of affiliates across the country, and conducts workshops and referral and donor programs.

In addition, the following organizations provide educational materials and other publications and products:

Children's Book-of-the-Month Club
National Braille Press
88 St. Stephen Street
Boston, MA 02115
(617) 266-6160

The Children's Braille Book-of-the-Month Club provides regular-print picture books with plastic braille over each page to members on a monthly basis. Individual books can also be ordered by nonmembers.

Exceptional Teaching Aids
20102 Woodbine Avenue
Castro Valley, CA 94546
(415) 582-4859

Exceptional Teaching Aids manufactures and distributes educational materials and equipment for visually impaired students, including tutorial and other educational software programs; braille materials for reading readiness, math readiness, and math practice; and books on cassette.

Howe Press
Perkins School for the Blind
175 North Beacon Street
Watertown, MA 02172
(617) 924-3434

Howe Press manufactures and sells the Perkins Brailler, as well as other tools, materials, and equipment for producing braille.

Twin Vision Lending Library
American Action Fund for Blind Children and Adults
18440 Oxnard Street
Tarzana, CA 91356
(818) 343-2022

Twin Vision Lending Library serves blind parents and blind children by lending Twin Vision Books and other braille publications written on the preschool to junior-high reading level. Twin Vision Books publishes children's books that combine print and braille on facing pages so that blind and sighted people can read together.

About the Contributors

Rona L. Pogrund, Ph.D., is a private consultant in visual impairment in Austin, TX; at the time of the institutes, she was associate professor, Department of Special Education, and director, Orientation and Mobility Training Program, California State University, Los Angeles. The co-author of a number of articles on such topics as preschool orientation and mobility and advocacy, she has also worked as an orientation and mobility specialist, teacher of visually impaired children, and special education administrator.

Diane L. Fazzi, M.Ed., is director, Orientation and Mobility Training Program, California State University, Los Angeles. She has worked as a teacher of blind and visually impaired children and an orientation and mobility specialist. She is currently completing a joint doctoral program with a focus on early childhood special education at California State University, Los Angeles, and the University of California, Los Angeles.

Jessica S. Lampert, M.A., O.T.R., is an orientation and mobility specialist and occupational therapist, Dallas Low Vision Clinic/Dallas Services for Visually Impaired Children. She has had extensive experience in working with young visually impaired children.

Tanni L. Anthony, Ed.S., is program coordinator, Blind/Visually Impaired Infant Program, Special Education Service Agency, Anchorage, AK.

Renee A. Cohen, Ph.D., is a clinical psychologist in private practice, West Los Angeles, CA; at the time of the institutes, she was consulting clinical psychologist, Center for the Partially Sighted, Santa Monica, CA.

Jane N. Erin, Ph.D., is assistant professor, Department of Special Education, University of Texas, Austin.

Karen M. Finello, Ph.D., is assistant professor of pediatrics, School of Medicine, University of Southern California, Los Angeles.

Robert L. Gordon, O.D., F.A.A.O., is an optometrist specializing in low vision rehabilitation in Encino, CA.

Nancy Hedlund Hanson, M.A., is a learning disability specialist, Santa Monica College, Santa Monica, CA; at the time of the institutes, she was program consultant, Foundation for the Junior Blind, Los Angeles, CA.

Lois Harrell, B.S., is coordinator/counselor, Childrens Vision Assessment Center, Department of Ophthalmology, University of California, Sacramento; at the time of the institutes, she was home counselor, Blind Babies Foundation, San Francisco, CA.

Sherwin J. Isenberg, M.D., is professor and vice-chairman, Department of Ophthalmology, Jules Stein Eye Institute, School of Medicine, University of California, Los Angeles.

Linda S. Kekelis, M.A., is a graduate student in special education at the University of California, Berkeley, and at San Francisco State University.

Shirley A. Kirk, M.A., is coordinator, Functional Vision Assessments, Visually Handicapped Program, Los Angeles Unified School District, Los Angeles, CA; at the time of the institutes, she was a teacher of visually impaired infants in the same district.

Cheryl I. Macon, M.S.W., is director, Infant/Parent Early Intervention Programs, Drew Child Development Corporation, Los Angeles, CA.

Sri J. Moedjono, M.D., is medical director, Harbor Regional Center for the Developmentally Disabled, Torrance, CA, and assistant clinical professor, Department of Pediatrics, Center for Health Sciences, University of California, Los Angeles.

Linda S. Orrante, M.S.W., L.C.S.W., is assistant director, Fresno County Department of Social Services, Fresno, CA; at the time of the institutes, she was program director, SENDEROS: Services for Latinos, Santa Monica, CA.

Ruth S. Pearce, M.A., is a private consultant and child development specialist in Los Angeles, CA.

Patricia Sacks Salcedo, M.A., is a teacher of visually impaired students, Blind Children's Learning Center, Santa Ana, CA; at the time of the institutes, she was an infant specialist, Foundation for the Junior Blind, Los Angeles, CA.

Patricia Taylor-Peters, M.A., is associate professor and director, Department of Special Education, University of LaVerne, LaVerne, CA; at the time of the institutes, she was principal, Los Angeles County Office of Education, Downey, CA.

Sheila Wolfe, M.A., O.T.R., is coordinator of educational programs, Assistive Device Center, California State University, Sacramento; at the time of the institutes, she was coordinator, Foundation for the Junior Blind Infant-Family Program, Los Angeles, CA.

Alana M. Zambone, Ph.D., is coordinator, International Outreach Services, Hilton/Perkins International Program, Watertown, MA; at the time of the institutes, she was national consultant in multiple disabilities and early childhood, American Foundation for the Blind, New York, NY.

"Training Personnel to Serve Visually Impaired and Multihandicapped Infants and Their Families" Institute Co-directors (*affiliations shown were current at the time of the institutes*)

Summer 1986:
Rona L. Pogrund, Ph.D., associate professor, Orientation and Mobility Training Program, California State University, Los Angeles.
Jenny Boyd, M.A., coordinator, Infant-Family Program, Foundation for the Junior Blind.

Summer 1987:
Rona L. Pogrund
Jessica S. Lampert, M.A., O.T.R., coordinator, Infant-Family Program, Foundation for the Junior Blind.

Summer 1988:
Rona L. Pogrund
Sheila Wolfe, M.A., O.T.R., coordinator, Infant-Family Program, Foundation for the Junior Blind.